Edward Hardingham

The Romance of Rahere

And Other Poems

Edward Hardingham

The Romance of Rahere
And Other Poems

ISBN/EAN: 9783744673914

Printed in Europe, USA, Canada, Australia, Japan

Cover: Foto ©Thomas Meinert / pixelio.de

More available books at **www.hansebooks.com**

THE ROMANCE OF RAHERE,

AND OTHER POEMS.

BY

EDWARD HARDINGHAM.

> ' But, for the unquiet heart and brain
> A use in measured language lies ;
> The sad mechanic exercise,
> Like dull narcotics, numbing pain.'
> TENNYSON—*In Memoriam.*

LONDON :

ELLIOT STOCK, 62, PATERNOSTER ROW, E.C.

1896.

To

W. R. MILLAR, Esq.,

MY OLD SCHOOLFELLOW AND LIFE-LONG FRIEND,

I offer this little Work,

IN LOVING RECOGNITION OF MANY

KINDNESSES.

January, 1896.

CONTENTS.

ALICE.

As it fell upon a day,
   I my thirst was slaking
At a brook beside the way,
   Leafy chalice making.

Came a maiden wondrous fair—
   Oh, my heart 'gan leaping !
Eyes of azure, golden hair,
   Feet like fairy's peeping.

' May I drink, good sir ?' she said,
   Oh, so sweetly smiling !
While she bent her pretty head,
   All my heart beguiling.

' First the fee !' I foolish cried,
   And the cup withholding ;
' Just a kiss.'   She, blushing, sighed :
   ' Not for thirst or scolding.'

Swiftly now the cup I lift,
  Meek repentance showing:
'Drink, sweet girl! Not mine the gift;
  'Tis Nature's own bestowing.'

Fearless now she drank, while I
  Draught of lover madness
Drank from blush and smile and sigh
  Of her grateful gladness.

Laughing now, she archly said,
  Void of fear or malice:
'Sir, the brook was Nature's aid,
  Yours the pretty chalice.'

'Keep it, then, fair maid,' I sighed,
  'With my heart to crown it.'
'Shalt not covet,' she replied;
  'Other maid may own it.'

'No; not so,' I cried in haste;
  'Love I scorned till lately.'
Rosy red, as Dian chaste,
  Stood she proud and stately.

'By the brook we both have drank
  Will you love me ever?'
On my knee I eager sank,
  'Sweet, till death shall sever.'

At the brook beside the way
  We our thirst a-slaking,
Deeper thirst we took that day,
  Lover pain and aching.

But the bells at break of morn
  Ring not long thereafter ;
Merry girls a bride adorn ;
  Shakes the roof with laughter.

Fairer bride ne'er gladdened sight ;
  Lovelier maiden never,
Bridal-robed, as angel bright,
  Plighted troth for ever.

Safely kept in frame of gold
  Lies the leafy chalice ;
Round its rim in letters bold
  Set the name of Alice.

SCORN.

Come, Ella ! the tyrannous town
  Forsake, with its madness.   Once more,
By river and upland and down,
  Come wander, as often of yore.
For, hateful, the city has soiled
  Our spirits, till, sordid and cold,
Of Godhood and manhood despoiled,
  They reck but of Mammon and gold.

Ah, curse on the dross that can mar
   God's image, so fair in its birth !
The spirit nor planet nor star
   Nor system can fetter to earth.
That love should die out of our hearts—
   Poor shadows, whose passing's a span—
And hell pride that lucre imparts
   Make man but the tyrant of man !

That the poor should be huddled as sheep
   In dens that a savage would scorn,
Where rotting and dying they weep—
   Ah, God, that we ever were born !
While the cry of the orphan goes up
   With the wail of the widow and maid ;
Of greed and oppression the cup
   We drain, Lord, with none to our aid.

Yet the rich they grow richer each day,
   While the famished must pilfer to feed,
And the cot of the peasant make way
   For the palace expanding of greed.
And the grain, the good gift of the God
   Who, overlong patient, restrains
His wrath, is bought up by the clod,
   Who, rich, must redouble his gains.

No matter that mothers must know
   The hunger-fiend pinching their breast ;
No matter that little ones go
   A-hungered and weeping to rest ;

No matter that fathers behold,
    Slow murdered, their offspring decay ;
No matter ! the demon of gold
    Unhinder'd must ride on his way—

Must ride on his way till the end
    Is reached in rebellion and war ;
Till hunger and misery blend
    Their forces with mercy afar ;
Till cities are reeking with blood,
    And red with the havoc of hate, .
That, age-long repressed, like a flood
    Bursts forth, unrelentless as Fate—

Bursts forth to avenge and requite.
    Woe, woe ! to the sowing that leads
To harvest of horror—the night
    Of Gomorrah o'erhanging your heads,
Ye rich, that the labourer's pay
    Begrudge, with the bread that in haste
He eats, lest a little less gay
    Ye go in your pride and your waste !

Away, then !   By river and wood,
    In the shade of the welcoming trees,
The mighty All-giver of good
    Shall whisper in brooklet and breeze
His peace to the spirits that mourn,
    As likest and nearest Himself,
The gold-greed accurst in His scorn,
    With worship of Mammon and pelf.

———

THE QUESTION.

A TALE OF THE PLAGUE AT HAARLEM.

Spring's flower-enamelled sceptre
    Assumed again, the land,
Delighted, wakes, and Winter,
    Withdrawing rigorous band,
Winds softly blow, while sunshine
    Fills all the leafing wood.
Flowers spring; birds sing and flitter,
    A careless, joyous brood.

The grass is pearled with daisies,
    Each bank with violets sweet;
The moss gold-fringed, most tempting
    The heather's yielding seat.
But, ah! of all the sweetest
    My lady, graceful laid
Beside the hurrying brooklet,
    Beneath the hornbeam's shade.

There lies she, thoughtful, dreaming;
    Her maiden fancies stray,
As pure as beam at dawning,
    Or dying even-ray.

Her sweet, sweet face is hidden,
  Her tresses falling low—
Rich cloud of silken sunlight—
. O'er brow as white as snow.

She wakes from dreams, and parting
  The hair-cloud from her face,
She smiles, and, smiling, beckons :
  My heart beats fever-pace.
'Come hither, sirrah, hither !
  Sir Poet, skilled of song !
Resolve the doubt that holds me—
  Has held me oft and long.'

I go, the spell of beauty
  My being thrilling through.
'So well !   Now sit beside me,
  And tell me, is it true
That woman's love, if milder,
  Is firm as Atlas range ?
Man's, summer hot, commingled
  With thunder-cloud and change ?'

' Nay, tell me first,' I answer,
  With lover-fire and thrill,
Her look so soft and wistful
  Enthralling mind and will—
'Say, first, what love you bear me,
  Then I can truly say,
Thrice that I love, and ever
  The more from day to day.

'Dost smile, my queen?   Then listen
    A tale I read of late,
Of noblest self-devotion
    To death for love's own sake.
The book lies in my bosom ;
    Shalt hear how men can die
At call of love, and dying,
    Deem death but ecstasy.'

Then I took the book from my breast, and read
    To my love in the woodland hollow
A tale of the brave and the faithful dead—
    Such faith would that all could follow !

On Haarlem town the sun shone brightly down—
Old Haarlem loved of labour and of art;
Mother of sons as brave as they that fought
The Persian host at Pylæ.   Glorious band
Of heroes, stubborn as the craggy pass,
They, dauntless, held against the millioned foe,
And, dead, yet held, a bleeding rampart heaped
Of sympathetic Death, so they might win
Their motherland a breathing-space for hope,
And gathering swift of all her warrior sons.

Such Haarlem's sons in fight ; nor famous less
In time of peace.   Fit consorts they of dames
And daughters fair as they that drew of old
Impassioned suitors out their paradise.
Of them, perchance, she sprang, sweet girl who sat
Within the Bloemen Tuin all ablaze

With glow of hyacinth close set, and gleam
Of tulips many-hued, and chaliced snow
Of Narcisse crimson-lipped—what flower more fair
In bloom-strewed Eden ?   Oh, that when I die
These wave above the grassy plat that keeps
My restful soul awhile !   So shall I dream
Again the dreams that flushed me when a boy,
Of wood and field, and babbling brook, and shade
Of forest giant, and the cuckoo note,
Now near, now far, like restless spirit lost
In depths of lacing boughs and ferny weed.

Within the garden sat the maid, her locks
Of sunny gold about her swelling breast—
Swelling with fancies sweet, of love and him
Who sat beside her drinking draughts of love
From out the limpid springs of her bright eyes—
Cerulean wells as clear and fair as e'er
Refreshed the bents on Ida's fertile hill.

Anon the maiden sighed.   'Cornelius, why
Such greed of fame ?   What is't but praise of them,
Maybe, that scorned thee living, or of them
That come long after, when the soul released
From earth nor heeds nor cares what mortal tongue
Bestows of praise or censure ?   Better far
Enjoy the day.   Am I not rich—is not
Our troth firm pledged ?   Ah, what were fame to me
Despoiled of love and lover ?'   Sudden now
Her tender eyes grew dim with veil of tears ;
Her boddiced bosom heaved ; her little hand
Sought his with wistful pressure.

To his lips
He raised it swift, then mild remonstrance made :
' Nay, Elsie—nay, dear love ! 't is love alone
That bids me follow fame and win renown.
Naught have I now to lay at beauty's feet
But love for love, and fame for burgher wealth.
The first, long since I gave ; the last shall come—
Wilt see my work ?   Enough is done to show
True artist and the master-skill that turns—
Wise magic far beyond mere wizard craft—
Dull wood and canvas into flush of life.
Van Ostade praises, brave Ruysdaal, too,
My master friend.   Come, Elsie, see the work !
'Tis Moses lifting up the brassy snake
'Mid crowd of plague-struck Hebrews !'

Elsie here
Grew pale, and trembling laid her pretty head
Upon her lover's arm.   ' How couldst thou choose
Such woeful subject ?   Even now 'tis said
The plague-fiend stalks unlet through Amsterdam,
And threats our gates.   Pray God no prophet seer
Be needed here to save a stricken folk !
Yet 't was foretold.   But Catherine hither now
Is come to bid me homeward.   Dear one, pray
No evil light on either !   All night long
I'll pray for thee that never plague may dog
Thy harmless footsteps.   Kiss me and farewell !'

That night the horror o'erleaped Haarlem's wall,
And raged like tigress 'venging slaughtered whelps.
A day ! and terror blanched each civic cheek.

A week! and wailing filled both cot and hall,
The city one vast lazar-house, and heaped
With loathsome victims.
      Hapless, Elsie now
Was smitten. What, to Death, her beauty rare,
Her virtue, or the fond parental care
That sought to shield her e'en from taint of ill?
The fiend was in the air. The very buds
And blossoms in the lonely Tuin felt
Its curse, and, sickening, drooped their heads and died.
A gloom hung over all. The sun, as sad
At sight of suffering all beyond relief,
Withheld its light; the moist earth reeked; the breeze
Kept off; no bird flew o'er the dying town,
Or beat its wing around Saint Bavon's spire.
Each thing that could forsook the fatal walls
Of Haarlem, yielded up to woe and death.

Of Elsie, hopeless smitten, ere the noon
Cornelius heard, as, mahl in hand, he stood
Before the growing offspring of his skill,
And, groaning, let his brush and palette fall.
Upon the wall was pendent crucifix,
Which, hasty snatched, he pressed against his lips.
'O Christ, whose pangs redeemed a God-doomed world,
Wilt Thou not save? Have mercy, mighty Lord,
Or let me share the ill Thou canst not heal.'

So prayed he madly. Then his fevered gaze
Fell on the picture. 'Dream of fame, farewell!
Full sure suggested by some voice of hell.

My Elsie dead, nor brush nor pigment more
I touch, but gladly share her virgin tomb.'

Not meant the deed, but in his frenzied clasp
The image broke.   He saw it with dismay
At first, then laughed as madmen laugh, and cried :
' And men can pray to thee, and kiss the limbs ;
A ruder touch than common thus can mar !
Prayer ! What is prayer? Did prayer keep out our
   walls
The bloody Spaniard when we fought for faith,
With honour of our mothers, sisters, wives,
And all things counted holy?   Can it snatch
One victim out the pest-fiend's ravenous maw,
Or save a harmless maid one torturous pang ?
To demon will the world is given o'er,
And hellish powers that sport and play with men,
Flesh puppets born to mis'ry !   Sickness, death—
The foes that dog man's footsteps—sorrow, shame,
His foreborn comrades.   Nuzzling in his breast
The viper Hope, that, cherished, double fang
Turns on her host ; while ever-callous Loss
Stands cruel by with lifted mall to smite
His bursting heart with scornful mocker-blow !'

So cried he frantic ; then, with firm resolve,
Ran out and on to dying Elsie's home.
The gate fast locked, he searched the garden wall.
A bough hung over.   All his strength he set
In one vast effort.   Leaping wildly up,
He clutched the friendly tree, and scaled the wall.

Now on toward the house. Death-silent all
The garden, court, and mansion. None came nigh
To chide or welcome, neither man nor maid.
Alone his footsteps filled the place with sound,
That answer made the pulsings of his heart
Tumultuous. Now the upper stair he climbed
To try each door. All opened ; none within,
But all disordered as from hasty flight.
Yet one remained, that fast ; he eager struck
A questioning blow against the sounding oak.
A heavy sigh made answer, with a cry,
Half moan, half question : ' Jesu, who is there ?
None are there in the house—all gone, all fled—
But I, plague-stricken, hopeless, left to die !'

A strange, fierce joy now filled Cornelius' breast ;
He even smiled the while he made reply :
' 'Tis I, Cornelius, come, my sweet, to share
Thy fate whate'er it be, or life or death.'
But Elsie shrieked. ' Ah, no, my love—ah, no !
Go back—go back ! Not love, but hate were mine
To slay by welcome what I treasure most ;
The very air is poisoned with my breath.
Go back, my own, my darling ! I can die.'

He would not, but with oft beseeching sought
To win him entrance, till she feebly cried :
' I cannot rise, dear love, and God be praised !
I cannot, or my woman heart might do
The deed my soul abhors !'

                              Now maddened quite
At sound of voice so loved, so full of pain,
He, furious, shook the door.   Too firm ; he spent
His strength in vain against the massy frame
And deep-set bolt.   Then came the heaven-sent thought—
The window !   Thereby I may enter in,
Too weak my love to bar my res'lute way.

Again within the garden, 'neath the trees,
He stood and scanned the windows.   ' This it is,
Beneath yon gable.   Ah, great God ! 'tis barred.'
But over all the wall a pear-tree grew,
And, all his soul on fire, he climbed the tree.
She helpless lay within upon her bed,
Beneath the casement.   Ah, those cruel bars !
To keep afar such matchless love and truth.
In vain with bleeding hands he wrenched and tore :
Too well the smith had wrought.   'Twas all in vain.

He wept with rage.   ' Ah, Elsie, Elsie ! now
For giant strength to tear these callous bolts
From out their stony sockets !'
                              Elsie heard,
And, moaning, turned her sore disfigured face
Toward the pane.   He groaned, such awful change
Was wrought upon her features, late so fair.
' My life !   Ah, me ! were mine the pain, so thou
Hadst 'scaped the scourge.   Yet will I share.'
                                        This said,
He broke the pane.   ' My queen, I cannot reach
That listless hand or those so tortured lips ;

The pain-drops on thy brow I may not kiss
Away with lover kisses, or sustain
Thy dying head upon my breaking heart.
But I can die with thee, and so o'erleap
The gulf of Time and barrier set between
The dead and living.'
                              Off the spreading tree
He brake a slender spray, whose leafy top
Yet bore a late-born blossom. To his lips
He set the bloom, then through the broken pane
Thrust in the spray. 'My sweet one, I have set
A kiss upon the bloom, for only thus
My lips may reach thee. Kiss thou in return.'

A spasm shook the dying maiden's form,
Her glazing eyes fast fixed upon the face,
So haggard, yet so faithful o'er her hung,
But at such unkind distance. In her hand,
With last brave effort urged of quenchless love,
She took the spray, scarce conscious that she did,
And set it softly on her deathly lips,
Then, weary sighing, slept to wake in bliss.

A moment gazed Cornelius on the dead,
Then, bitter smiling, kissed the pearly bloom,
So pure to sight, yet bearing in its depths
Plague-boon of death. Again and yet again
He kissed it, gazing ever on the face
Of her he loved so fondly and so well,
Until he felt the fever in his blood,
And knew the poison raging in his veins.

Yet still he clung to tree and bar, and still
He spake the dead, with dauntless smile and tone :
' My own ! my own !   I come, and soon !   I feel
Already at my heart the fiery thrill.
Ere night, my queen—ere night, I come to thee.'

So clung he long time, whispering words of love
As she could hear, till, strength at end, he fell
Upon the turf beneath, but ever held
The spray tight clenched within his hand, and kissed
The kindly bloom, and ever bent his gaze
Up to the casement, and so gazing died.

   *   *   *   *   *

No more I read.   My Ella's face was hid
Again behind her veil of silken hair ;
But on her hands I saw the piteous tears
Fall, like to April shower.   What need to ask ?
I knew her question answered to the full.

PERDIDI DIEM !

PERDIDI DIEM !   Nigh a baker's shop
A man stood wistful—in his arms a child
Asleep of weariness.   Alas ! beguiled
By pleasant converse with a friend, to stop
I thought not, but passed by—Perdidi diem !

Perdidi diem !   After, at my meal,
My pets about me jealous each of each,
A weary face, more eloquent than speech,
Rose up, Egyptian guest.   I could but feel
The sting of thoughtlessness—Perdidi diem !

Perdidi diem ! ' Evermore the poor
Ye shall have with you.' Thus the Lord of all.
Ah, God, how oft they look, they sigh, they call !
We pass them careless by, or close the door.
Forgive me, Lord, for oft—Perdidi diem !

Perdidi diem ! Down the village street
A-dust with summer heat, and broader road,
Self-judged and self-condemned, I eager strode ;
A mile, then two, and three, yet could not greet
Again the wanderer pair—Perdidi diem !

Perdidi diem ! Sorrowful at heart
Returning home, I vowed no more for shame
Ill felt, or pride, or selfish ease, the claim
Of outcast to repel, or hunger smart
Of poverty to quicken, lest one day
The God alike of rich and poor should say,
Tu perdidisti diem, servant Mine.

Non perdidisti diem, dost thou lift
A wormling out the path of hurrying men ;
Dost save a moth from flame ; the guiltless wren
Release from snare, or straying beetle shift
Back to its burrow ; but at close of day
Canst peaceful sleep to dream thy Lord doth say,
Non perdidisti diem, servant Mine !

ST. MARK'S EVE.

I.

And who, then, with me in the chancel to-night
  Will watch, while the silver-rayed queen
Slow rides through the night in her vesture of light
  O'er hilltop and valley between?
While solemn the tempest sweeps through the firwood,
  And spectre and goblin and elve
Come forth from the gloom of sepulchre and tomb
  At boom of the turret at twelve!

For they that the vigil of blessed St. Mark
  Dare keep at the holy rood-screen,
Strange vision shall see ere the morrowing be—
  Most wondrous apparence, I ween.
For all they of Thoydon the weary year through
  That perish by land or by sea,
At midnight must pass through the churchyard to Mass
  With their priest and his acolytes three.

Oh, fair beyond telling was Margaret Clare
  Who bade to that vigil unblest;
Her forehead was bold, while her tresses of gold,
  Wind-frolicked, kissed bosom and breast.

Her eyes they were limpid and blue as the wave
  That, breezeless and laid to repose,
In soft southern bay at the close of the day
  Like amethyst glistens and glows.

High-hearted she came from the coppice, her hands
  Befilled with the spoils of the wood—
With daffodils pale and anemones frail,
  And cuckoo-buds redder than blood.
Queen-crowned with a chaplet of daisies she stood—
  'Twas plaited by Laura Lestrange,
The maid at her feet : who so winsome and sweet
  As Laura of Coopersale Grange?

'And I then !—I also ! And, Margaret, I !'
  Her comrades made answer with glee ;
Save Rosamond, pale as the luce of the vale,
  Who, trembling, knelt down at her knee.
And ' Sister, dear sister,' she earnest replied ;
  ' Forbear ! oh, forbear now your quest !'
So pleaded the maid as her forehead she laid
  In terror on Margaret's breast.

But Margaret, laughing, ' My bonny white Rose,
  Thou ever wert troubled with fear
For me, from the day of our sisterly play—
  Sweet Rose without rival or peer !
But happen what may, in the chancel to-night
  I watch till the dawning of day.
So they now that dare in my vigil may share,
  And they that are fearful may stay.'

But Rosamond, sighing, uplifted her head,
  And sadly her sister she kist ;
Yet scarcely could see, for the fast-falling sea
  Of sorrow, love's soul-springing mist ;
And, clinging, entreated in tremulous tone :
  ' Dear sister, if any must go,
Let me be the one, for no peril I'll shun
  To save thee from danger or woe.'

' Not so.   None shall venture for sparing of me,'
  Said Margaret, proud as the day
At morn, that with beam and with fervour and gleam
  Recks not of the dying away.
' I go, and go fearless ; but, Rosamond, you
  Shall not, lest misfortune befall ;
So stay you and pray till the breaking of day,
  And carol of lark at its call.'

II.

Not yet from her couch in the lonely firwood
  The moon had arisen serene,
Though silvery-white was the canopy bright
  That hung o'er the slumbering queen.
And soft was the breeze as the murmur of harp,
  Or fountain's Eolian strain,
Or sighing of maid with her cherry lips laid
  To those of her passionate swain.

And dark was the chapel enshrouded in trees
  O'erhanging the grave-chequered knoll ;
The clang of its bell, as the midnight befell,
  Like knell for a moribund soul.

But bravely the maid with her tryst-fellows three
  Hid up in the oaken rood-loft,
With fond arms entwined as their heads they inclined
  Full oft to her whispering soft.

Hush ! hush ! for the hour it is knelling.   And see
  Yon light with its corpse-kindled gleam !
The chancel is gray with its shadowless ray ;
  It spreads over pillar and beam.
And list, too, the organ beginning to roll !
  But softly ! and see, too, the bread
Is set with the cup of which only may sup
  The priest at the Mass of the dead.

They fearfully watching, the prodigy grew,
  And ever the requiem rolled
Its withering strain, while again and again
  The passing-bell drearily tolled.
And see now, wide opened of grave-quickened hand,
  The portal is noiselessly flung,
As slow on the wall, to the requiem's fall,
  The bannerols mournfully swung.

And weirdly the glamour streamed onward, and lit
  The yews and the cypresses low,
Each sorrow-twined wreath, with the gravestone beneath,
  Ablaze with the marvellous glow.
And awful ! see now in the fascinous light
  That ghostly funereal band,
The pathway upled by their priest at their head,
  Close now to the charnel-house stand !

And babelings were there that as yet were unborn,
  With wives that as yet were unwed ;
And schoolmaidens fair that unhappy should share
  The grave with the silver-thatched head.
And all as they halted the sign of the cross
  Made slowly on bosom and brow ;
Then silently came, while the space-filling flame
  Shone fiercely on headstone and bough.

Still onward, while, swelling, the weird organ-strain
  Was sad as the wail of the wave
That sweeps o'er the deck of the rock-splintered wreck,
  And beats at the mariner's grave.
Now halting, close gathered, beneath the rood-screen,
  They kneel while their passionless priest,
His antiphons said, incenses the bread
  And wine for the marvellous feast.

Oh, dauntless as eagle was Margaret Clare ;
  What dread in her bosom might hide,
Who never had known a desire that had grown
  To sin against virginal pride ?
For often alone with her staghound at night
  She walked in the forestal glade,
No fear at her heart though her comrade should start
  And bay at the quivering shade.

But now she knew terror, and clung to the rood,
  Her forehead embracing its feet ;
It shook with her clasp and the fire of her grasp,
  Her bosom's impetuous beat.

But bravely she battled the fear in her soul,
  And conquered—her conquest how sore !
Less happy than they, her companions, who lay
  A-swoon at her feet on the floor.

For three of those ghastly life shadows she knew,
  And one was child Laura, that lay
Already as dead, in her horror and dread,
  Her face marble, pallid, and gray ;
The others—ah, God ! for the pang in her breast !—
  The last of the phantomic train :
A youth and a lass ; 'twas herself that did pass
  With him that was sailing the main.

The gold on his shoulder was fleckered with blood,
  The blue was commingled with red
By broiderer Death, when the laborous breath,
  Fate-bidden, the conqueror fled.
And she : on her bosom the marshweed lay dank ;
  The clotted blood hung in her hair ;
Her kirtle was wet, and her gaze it was set,
  With the drowning girl's agonized stare.

But either yet turned on the other a look
  Of love, all unspeakable still—
· Though he had his grave 'neath the far-sounding wave,
  And she in the church-shadowed hill.
And peaceful, hands clasping, together they knelt,
  While wondrous the melody rolled
Through chancel and aisle, as slowly the while
  The sanctus-bell solemnly tolled.

Now slowly the celebrant lifted the cup,
　　And signed the blest sign in the air;
Then worshipped the Host, while Margaret crost
　　Her breast at the measureless glare
That burst from the chalice and patine, and fell
　　Aflame on her bosom and brow,
As low at the screen, and as yet all unseen,
　　She knelt with the phantoms below.

Was 't hazard or purpose?   Her lover looked up;
　　He saw her, and bending his head
With unearthly grace, did he show her a place
　　Beside him—a place with the dead!
Ah, wondrous life-ruler! Fate monarch! Ah, Love!
　　Thou victor and spoiler of Death!
No terror she knew, but undauntedly drew
　　To the shade of her lover beneath.

The organ note sank to a murmurous fall;
　　The glamour redoubled its light;
As calm in its sheen, all untroubled, serene,
　　Like to star in the tiar of night,
She came to the side of her lover; and, lo!
　　The shadow departed that dwelt
Beside him erewhile, as with welcoming smile
　　He bent, while she silently knelt.

And calmly beside him she knelt, and her soul
　　Went up to Jehovah in prayer:
'On earth or in heav'n, my troth-pledge is giv'n
　　To him, and his hazard I share.

Forgive, if thus loving I sin, Lord, for love
  Of Thee is begotten alone ;
I do but keep troth, assoil Thou then both ;
  Let Mass for misdoing atone.'

Now drew the priest near ; all untroubled she bore
  His death-gaze, as, crossing her hands,
She shared with the rest, in the Sacrament blest,
  That the Christ-God His people commands.
And sudden her spirit, complacent, beheld,
  In faithful foreshadowing clear,
The doom that should be, upon land and on sea,
  To each ere the death of the year.

Mass ended, the pageant slow faded away ;
  And, people and celebrant gone,
Night's cloud-girdled queen, with her crystalline sheen,
  Looked down on the maiden alone.
And placid its beam through the checkering pane
  Came flooding the chorestal floor,
Like angel of light, with a message of might
  To spirits earth-wearied and sore.

And, lo ! to her fancy the face of the Christ,
  Thorn-crowned, in the traceried frame,
Shone out in the ray in a mystical way,
  With love and compassion aflame.
And tearful she worshipped : ' O Fountain of love !
  Grant now I may service Thee well,
Whate'er may befall, till Thy welcoming call,
  And close of life's wearisome spell !'

Thereafter uprising, she went to the stair,
    And, climbing its newel-stone steep,
'Wake, Catherine, wake! or my kisses shall break
    The charm of thy merciful sleep!
And, Laura, dear comrade, unconscious of fate,
    Awake! for thy lifehood is fleet.
Rise, Emily, rise! we must home ere the skies
    Morn's embassy lovingly greet.'

And sighing they woke at the call of the voice,
    So passionless, tranquil, and clear;
Untroubled they woke, but as memory broke,
    They trembled and murmured with fear.
But cheerful she chid them: 'Ah, cowards! afraid
    Of naught but the silver moonbeam;'
But nothing they said, as they eagerly fled
    The scene of their terrible dream.

But Margaret held in her embrace a hand—
    'Twas Laura's, full clammy, and cold—
And lifted it oft to her bosom so soft,
    Yet ever so dauntless and bold.
And hastening onward, ere long there shone out
    The lights from the hill-topping hall;
But bodingly howled in their kennels, and growled,
    The dogs, as they sped by the wall.

And Rosamond springing to Margaret's arms,
    For gladness her pearly tears fell.
'And what did you see?' did she ask in her glee;
    But Margaret nothing would tell;

But, gently caressing the eager young face,
  Uplifted in love to her own :
' Ask nothing, my sweet ! for I may not repeat
  What to me was in secrecy shown.'

The others but little could proffer, so soon
  Their senses by terror opprest :
The gleaming could tell, with the slow-swinging bell,
  The organ—but naught of the rest.
And morning came filling the landskip with light,
  And evening succeeded to day ;
But ne'er from each heart did remembrance depart,
  Or sorrow surrender its sway.

III.

Oh, Margaret Clare she was wealthy and great,
  Far-stretching her manors and wide,
And if she were proud, e'en detraction allowed
  Her noble, spite glozing of pride.
'Twas pride that, disdaining the grudging of greed,
  Ne'er snatched from the few-friended poor,
The way-gotten plot or the shingle-thatched cot
  That crouched at the edge of the moor.

And often, nor waiting for word of distress,
  She went through the welcoming street,
A smile for each door, with a gift for the poor,
  And the children she lingered to meet.
For lonely she dwelt in her hall on the hill—
  All dead were her kith and her kin,
Save Rosamond gay, whose feet the whole day
  Made life with their musical din.

And both were troth-plighted.   But Margaret's heart
   Was won by Sir Reginald Hood,
Awatch on the main for the galleons of Spain,
   Curse-laden of carnage and blood.
He homeward returning, the clamorous bells
   Would tell of the wedding and feast—
The wide-opened hall and the fleet-footed ball,
   With largess for greatest and least.

But now there came tidings from over the sea
   Of victory wrought on the main,
Of battle by night and the Spaniards in flight,
   But also—Sir Reginald slain !
And softly, long doubtful, they ventured the tale ;
   She heard them as one that hath share
No longer in life—in its joy or its strife,
   Its happiness, misery, care.

But only she went to the chancel at noon,
   And knelt on the knee-furrowed stone,
And gazed on the face of the Christ-God whose grace
   Gives peace to the weary alone,
Oft pleading : ' O Lamb of the aye-living God,
   Who bleeding didst die, and for me,
Ah ! comfort me now, for in sorrow I bow,
   And lift up my soul unto Thee.'

And summer departing, the mellowing mist
   Came up from the stream-threaded lea ;
Its vaporous breath, like funereal wreath,
   Hung ghostly on hedgerow and tree.

And borne on its pinions, death-fretted, it brought,
  Relentless, fate-message for one ;
And Margaret sighed, for at Hallowmas-tide
  Was Laura's life-voyaging done.

And kissing the maiden's cold forehead, full low
  She whispered : ' Not long now, and I
Shall sleep by thy side, nor shall foolishly chide
  The days that they sluggishly fly.'
And all about marvelled that never a tear
  She shed, nor complaining let fall,
For love-dream at end, or for loss of the friend
  She cherished as dearest of all.

'Twas eve of the Mass of the Saviour—blest time
  Of peace upon earth and in air ;
The louvre bells rang, and the carollers sang
  Their songs on the terracèd stair.
And Margaret listened beside the yule-fire,
  A smile on her high-thoughted face—
The summons so near, with the death of the year,
  That now was departing apace.

' Oh, worship the King !' so the carollers sang ;
  Her spirit went up with the strain
To regions of light, where in measureless might
  The King of all kinglets doth reign.
And ' " Nowell," ' she murmured ; ' Thou all-gracious
    God !—
  " Nowell " on this heart-thrilling eve—
Thou Well-spring of love that of mercy didst move
  Man's burden to prove and reprieve !'

And after she summoned the carollers in,
  And tankard and wassail went round,
While nigh to her knee was the eldest of three
  Whose father in autumn was drowned.
And laying her hand on the chorister's head,
  She blessed him, and bade him beware ;
True son he should show to his mother, nor know
  A thought that she never might share.

They gone with her largess, she sat by the blaze,
  Her thought with the two that were dead ;
Till Rosamond came, and, with pleasure aflame,
  Bent mirthfully over her head.
And suddenly circling her neck with her arms,
  Her face she drew close to her own—
' Oh, far-away queen, with the morrow, I ween,
  Must pleasure for brooding atone.'

And ' Harold is going,' she said with a blush ;
  ' But early to morrow at morn
Is coming with Kate ; and all's well, we will skate
  On the lake by the three-parted thorn.'
Then Margaret rose ; and her sister for long
  Remembered, with yearning and pain,
The look in her face, with her silent embrace,
  Her kiss, and her lingering strain.

And presently taking the youth by the hand,
  ' A word with you, Harold, aside.
Nay, Rosamond, nay ! What to Harold I say
  From you I do purposely hide.'

Then told she the tale of that marvellous night—
  He speechless through grief and dismay—
That she on her bier ere the close of the year
  Must lie in sepulchral array.

And straitly she charged him to treasure his bride—
  Be husband and brother in one,
For the sake of the friend, who, her sorrow at end,
  For aye had her rapture begun.
Then sisterly parting she set on his cheek,
  His sorrow so truthfully shown ;
'Twas lofty-souled youth, whose honour and truth
  She knew and could trust as her own.

'And when thou art master, and fillest my place,
  Think oft of the poor and the old :
For life is at best but a struggle for rest,
  And gratitude better than gold.
And he who that garners is richer by far
  Than he, the false steward of God,
Of charity bare, whose wealth is a snare,
  And misapplied talent a rod.

'And now fare thee well ! for to-night I must ride
  To Lambourne. Nurse Alice would grieve
Full sore did she miss of her foster-child's kiss
  And God-speed ere ending of eve.
Good-bye, then. Come early, for Rosamond's sake.
  Yet see in this oaken bureau
My testament set, with a word for my pet—
  God lighten her burden of woe !'

IV.

Most lovely the even, as Margaret rode
  To Lambourne by hedgerow and lane ;
And lustre streamed down from the Lyre and the Crown,
  And the Dogs by the Waggoner's Wain.
And Victor, her staghound, ran joyous, and oft
  Would leap in his glee at the horse ;
Then, bounding off, bark, to pursue in the dark
  The hare through the snow and the gorse.

And firm was the seal of the frost on the road,
  On brooklet and millstream and pond ;
The ice it gleamed white, in the nebulous light,
  On river and marshes beyond.
And sparkling the snowdrift lay deep in the dell,
  And under the slant of the hedge ; '
While keen the wind blew, as, the osier-beds through,
  Wild sighing it snarled at the sedge.

The welkin was loud with the musical clang
  Of the bells in their turreted lair ;
The song and the din of the broad-gabled inn
  Swept merrily out on the air ;
While lightsome the lilt of the viola rose,
  With harp in the many-voiced street ;
And cheery each tongue with a welcoming rung,
  Where neighbours and relatives meet.

Now reaching the cottage, she gave up the rein
  To one that ran out to the gate ;
Where also the dame in her eagerness came,
  The light on her white-kerchiefed pate.

And clasping her charge to her motherly breast,
  She kissed her in pride and in glee :
'My darling is late, but as steadfast as fate ;
  I knew that her face I should see.'

And restful awhile in the snow-covered cot
  She lay in the arms of her friend ;
The moments how fast do they speed !—they are past !
  'Now hallow me, Christ, to the end.'
A motherly clasp and a lingering kiss,
  But hearken her whinnying horse !
A smile from the dame, and good-bye ! But she came
  In an hour to her bosom a corse.

All heedless she rode, for her heart it was full
  Of peace, and her spirit away
From pulsing of life with its turmoil and strife,
  Its prison and fetters of clay.
Unhindered her palfrey returned by a road,
  A way she was wonted to choose
When summer had drunk at the river, and shrunk
  Its waters to streamlet and ooze.

But ere that the car of the snow-cradled king
  Rolled down on the quivering ground,
All over the mead had the waters outspread,
  Full soon to be fettered and bound.
Ice-fettered and bound at a breath of the king,
  And rigid for many a rood,
The ice-ichor gleamed, where the bulrushes streamed
  Acrest of the meadow-spread flood.

3

A star now a-sudden flashed out in the night,
  And system and planet grew dim
In blaze of the world, death-bidden and hurled
  To ruin, restoreless and grim.
And, startled, the palfrey sprang forward !   In vain
  Awak'ning, she caught at the rein ;
Regardless he fled, and the fire from his tread
  Leapt out of the crystalline plain.

And stumbling of terror, he brake the ice through,
  And rolled in the turgidous flood ;
She fell from her seat—with his adamant feet
  He struck—she was blinded with blood !
And clutching full wildly at saddle and band,
  She clutched in her anguish in vain ;
But fainting could hear, and her covert anear,
  The carollers chaunting again.

' Adeste fideles,' they carolled, the strain
  All solemnly blessing the air ;
She echoed the word : ' I come, then, dear Lord !
  Hail, Babe of the manger-cratch bare !'
And sullen the waters closed over her head ;
  But joyous her spirit returned
To land of its birth, as the trammels of earth,
  Ecstatic, it evermore spurned.

His foothold regaining, the fallen horse smote
  The ice till he stood on the bank ;
But Victor loud bayed, and his mistress essayed
  To reach where she silently sank.

For swiftly he plunged in the black-bosomed pool
  And catching her dress with his teeth,
He drew her to shore, his companion no more
  By hamlet or woodland or heath.

And ever he bayed, and he bayed till the night
  Was full of his sorrowful cry,
As, crouched in the sedge, he kept watch at the edge
  Of the river his mistress anigh.
And, wond'ring, the carollers ceased in their song,
  And hearkened again and again ;
Then followed the sound, till their lady they found,
  A corpse on the treacherous plain.

And weeping they lifted her out of the weed,
  And bearing her slow to the cot,
Dame Alice drew nigh, with a terrible cry :
  ' Ah, God, is Thy mercy forgot ?'
Then kissing in frenzy the blood-oozing brow,
  And lips that yet lovingly smiled,
She laid on her breast the dead maiden to rest,
  As oft when a light-hearted child.

At daybreak full early the ringers came forth,
  And mad was each clangorous bell,
Until the tale spread of their liege lady dead,
  When jubilance ended in knell.
And after was offered, with sighing and tears,
  The Christ-mass ; and service was sung
By lips that with pain but essayed the refrain,
  Their hearts all too bitterly wrung.

But dead she yet lived, and her wishes were law
 Long after in cottage and hall :
For she dwelt in each heart as a presence apart
 From death and the funeral-pall.
And years they drew by, but unceasing her tomb
 Was bright with the flowerets sweet
She loved as a maid, and by Rosamond laid
 With tears at her Margaret's feet.

But none ever after dare venture within
 The churchyard at vigil of Mark,
And children still run from its precincts, and shun
 Its causey at falling of dark.
For still it is whispered at midnight the door
 Swings ope, and the anthem is sung,
As slowly to Mass in the chancel doth pass
 That priest with his moribund throng.

———

THE WISH.

How happy I, had Fortune willed
    For me a roof in wooded glen :
Mine own—remote from stir, and filled
    With goodly books of goodly men ;
Oft read, oft pondered, laid to heart,
Sure friends no hap of ill can part !

How sweet to bid the jarring town
    Farewell, and calm in leafy cot
Untroubled move ; at night lie down
    World-aims, world-wishes all forgot ;
With never thought for morn but this :
Awakening brings return of bliss !

Ye winds, that wake the woodland strings
    To harmony, most sweet at night !
Ye thymy banks ! ye purling springs,
    That glist'ning glide like threads of light !
Ye birds, as free as thought, that rove
At will, or warbling shake the grove !

Ah me ! might I but mate with you,
    With you your harmless pleasures prove ;
Bid sense, and strife, and care adieu,
    Henceforth in nobler manhood move ;
Drawn close to Nature's breast, and kept
From snares, too late bewailed, bewept.

WINTER-EVE.

GOOD-LACK ! now day and task are done,
  Come master, maid, or peasant ;
We'll share around the well-set board
  Its store of junkets pleasant.
The snow bends low the spruce-fir bough,
  And cumbers beam and rafter ;
We'll shake it down ere long, I trow,
  With song and shout and laughter.

Our ingleside is bright and wide,
  Without there's blast and bluster ;
Come nearer, lads, there's room enow,
  Nor stand, nor stare, nor fluster.
Come sit and smoke, and jest and joke,
  While Sue with noisy clatter
Clears all away, while Spot and Tray
  Growl over greasy platter.

The mazer cup, oft filled, shall pass
  From hand to hand the fleeter
For kiss and sip of cherry lip,
  That makes the cup the sweeter;
While each the lass he favours toasts,
  And sighs and smiles and blushes,
Tell tales, and tempt to jig and dance
  Amid the cornflag rushes.

Then hoodman blind, each artful maid
　By laughter place betraying—
Sly things that shriek at lover grasp,
　And kiss, false fear essaying ;
Till, weary, gathered once again
　About the sere log blazing,
Relate the newest village feat,
　Or town-brought tale amazing.

Or tell of hag, and witch, and fay,
　And him that roams the heather,
All headless thorough bush and brake
　By night whate'er the weather ;
Of Dick that haunts the farmhouse hill,
　And Kate that fills the hollow
With drowning cries, and him that flies,
　Werewolf, while hellhounds follow.

So tell, while Joan and Kitty draw
　Their sweethearts' side the nearer,
Assured by circling arm—sweet life !
　Than lover clasp, what's dearer?
Now stay who will, the maids retire
　To rest, but all together—
Here's health to those that keep within,
　And those that brave the weather !

LILIAN LANE.

I.

'Twas dawn in Waltham Holy Cross, what time
    The Mass was sung for Harold, hapless king,
Forsworn and fall'n on Senlac's field sublime,
    His raven standard earthward fluttering,
With bloody fold, where, victory denied,
The royal brethren sank, and dauntless died.

For him, betrayed of fortune, what so well
    Became as death, and rest within the fane
His largess founded?   Oft the woful knell,
    Slow rung of monken hand, should wake again
In patriot breast the warrior flame, and chide
Lethargic hate that brooked tyrannic pride.

'Twas dawn within the minster.   Vast and fair
    Loomed chauntry, aisle, and chapel, dimly seen
Through gleam of shrine-set taper, or the flare
    Of cresset swung the transept arch between;
O'er all a glamour lay, with shadowy light
Adown the nave from brass-laid pillar bright.

For gloom prevailed, for all the Eastern gate
   Stood ope, unlatched at blithe Aurora's call ;
For all through pane, of servile Flemish state,
   The purpled radiance softly 'gan to fall
O'er shrine and tomb, and costly parquet pave,
And prayerful slab o'er crosiered abbot's grave.

Through pillared nave, and broad triforium span,
   By sculptured stall and rood of Bethlehem,
Rich gift of angel hand, the pleading ran,
   ' Eternam ei dona requiem,'
With retinue of echoes, whose refrain
Renewed the plaint again and yet again.

Sonorous now as when the wind-swept sea
   Resents storm's embrace, wildly strong and rude ;
Now sweetly sweet as when some moorland tree
   Pours forth at eve complaint of solitude ;
The Mass went on till all the quivering air,
Of pain grown voiceful, swelled the fervent pray'r.

Now paled the light of altar-taper, while
   The blazoned casement overhead grew bright
With beam of day.   Within the arching aisle
   Night sullen lingered, till increasing light
Renewed the war, and drave him thence, for all
   Support of pier and portal, screen and wall.

His Mass at end, the monk arose and closed
   His well-worn missal clasped with clasp of gold
Then slowly turned him, where the king reposed
   In tomb of porph'ry, richly wrought of old
With carving quaint, and bright mosaic stone
Of turquoise, agate, marble, chalcedone.

' Infelix Harold !' murmured he, his gaze
   Upon the legend, simple, gleaming red
On scroll of gold, that shone amid the blaze
   Of kindling light which all the shrine o'erspread
From nearer casement, where the glowing pane
Portrayed the king in conflict with the Dane.

' Infelix ?   No !   Unhappy he that spoils
   God's Church on earth, pretending hate of crimes
So like his own, they seem but counterfoils
   Of his own royal passions.   Evil times
Were thine indeed, O warrior earl, but still
Thou diedst a king, nor brooked tyrannic will

' In self or other.   Thine the nobler meed—
   A warrior's death—than his, whom foul disgrace
Pursues, the while he thinks to cover greed
   With fierce rebuke of ill in lesser place ;
Whose vices grow, till victims hourly plead
O'erpatient Heaven for judgment on his head.'

So said the monk.   Yet while he mournful spake,
  Upon his brow day's first full radiance fell.
'Twas healing touch. His face grew calm. 'So break,'
  He softly said, ' God's morrowings after spell
Of darkness and disfavour.   I will trust
Him though He slay, for all His ways are just.

' His ways are just.   He chastens to reform
  Alone, and metes but scanty meed of wrath.
His Church shall show the fairer for the storm,
  Though trembling now as reed in tiger path ;
Not yet the dirge of sacred truth is sung,
Not yet faith's knell by hands unholy rung.'

Now thoughtful turning where the organ stood,
  But waiting touch of skilful master hand
To fill the fane with sweet harmonic brood
  Of music tuneful as seraphic band,
Here sat he down to lose in restful strain
Distractive thought and sting of viper pain.

Awhile he played ; then sudden at his side
  Brake forth a song surpassing rich and clear ;
He mournful smiled, alone such tuneful tide
  Could flow, he knew, from him that warbled near—
A youth, a lad of lofty look, and hair
Of gold, that streaming fringed his surplice fair.

Like lark uplift on humid wing, and lost
  In flood of song, and cloud of morning gold,
The lad sang on from placid heart, untost
  By wave of tempest passion, or the cold
Recoil of stern repression. Sweeter song
Before ne'er swept the minster aisle along.

'Twas ancient hymn, oft sung with bated breath
  In cave and catacomb by trembling tongue,
While Death stood listening by, and fiery wreath
  Of martyrdom already overhung
The singers' heads, with spirit hands unseen
Stretched out to bless, or cheer, or intervene.

And playing on, yet softly, till the song
  Was done, and all the echoing aisles were still,
The monk beheld in visioned bliss the throng
  Of white-robed witnesses that life and will
Laid at their Master's feet—beheld, and smiled
To think how pain awhile had him beguiled,

Of faith and hope, their comrade, yet, of earth,
  Like them foredoomed to sorrow, trial, loss.
Himself again, thrice blessed prayer had birth :
  ' My God, like Thee, so may I bear the cross
And flaunting reed, else never victor palm ;
Know stripes and thorns, else never heavenly balm.'

So prayed the monk, his head upon his breast,
   His eyes o'ercast by sorrow's filmy frieze;
His song at end, the chorister caressed
   The tear-stained hand that idly grasped the keys;
And 'Father Abbot, why thus sad?' he said;
'Why weep you thus, and droop your holy head?

'The morn is fair—how fair! the minster gay '
   With newborn radiance; all without is bright
And careless glad at coming of Dan Day;
   See how yon tapers blink amid the light,
Their pigmy glory lost amid the flood
Of flame old Titan pours o'er screen and rood.

'Within the cloister, hark the tuneful din!
   My song has stirred to emulance of skill .
The fleet-winged brood, that often venture in
   The church at prime or vespers, ling'ring still
To learn, methinks, some inkling of the strain
We sing, to sing it to their mates again.'

The abbot smiled, a weary smile; then slow
   And mournful spake, his hand upon the bright
And clustering curls that decked his scholar's brow:
   'Can that be fair, dear lad, that turns to night
Day's golden hope, and scatters fear and gloom
O'er all the land, with swift and cruel doom

'Of death to those too faithful to accept
  A tyrant's will in place of holy trust?
And all, forsooth, that sin and wrong have crept
  Betimes among us, as they will and must
While men are men, else wherefore watchful pray'r,
Or priest, or Mass, or instant Christian care?

'Firm stand these walls, in pride of strength severe
:   Yon burnished panes diffuse effulgent ray;
Yon roof shows fair, as beauty naught need fear
  At builder hand.   Ah, me! ah, woeful day!
A little while and all shall ruined lie:
Church, cloister, choir, in shapeless misery!

'E'en now the king's commissioners set forth,
  And I must yield them strict accompt of all
I have in charge, of great or lesser worth,
  Nor dare refuse for dread of bloody fall;
Woe's me! that age should coward manly will,
And heav'n so near, earth prove more potent still.

'So am I sad, dear child; yet not that I
  No more shall sit in seat of godly men,
Or mitred rule.   An old worn man, I fly
  Distractive parley for the quiet pen,
And calm of cloistral cell.   Enough for me
God-given scope for Christian charity!

' Yet sing again. Nor, Francis, e'er forget
  Old Abbot Fuller, how he taught thee well
To use thy gift of song, nor e'er regret
  Forsaken bed at call of convent-bell ;
Sing yet again, before the doomstroke fall,
And voiceless ruin brood in choir and stall !

' Thou canst not, child, thy soul so disarrayed,
  And voice and speech suffused in guileless tears ?
Then be it so ! Together we have prayed—
  Our morrowing task at end, with all thy fears—
Full oft at yonder shrine. So kneel again
And holy Mary grant surcease of pain !'

Oh, fleet-winged prayer, celestial courier,
  Outspacing space, impassioned pursuivant
Of weary man to tireless Arbiter
  Of all, enshrined in sevenfold firmament !
Be mine to pray when care and grief oppress,
Or summer joys entice with loveliness !

Be mine to pray when morning's pinions cleave
  Resistless way through night's disparting veil ;
And mine to pray what time reposeful eve
  Her peaceful mantle casts o'er crest and dale,
In hopeful youth, proud prime, and av'rous age,
Be mine to pray all through life's pilgrimage !

II.

Where laggard Lea disparts her pleasant stream,
    And wraps the Waltham meads in soft embrace,
Young Francis strayed ; and, as in mocking dream
    Oft exiles see the roof-tree of their race,
So gazed the lad with sad and wistful eyes
Beyond the stream, where church and convent rise.

The crime complete, already spoiler hands
    Mad havoc wrought within the goodly fane ;
Already, slave to callous greed's commands,
    Unlettered violence won unhallowed gain ;
While sledges smote incessant, and the clang
Of pick and bar through crypt and cloister rang.

Down all ! down all !   Down choir magnifical,
    With shrine and tomb, and matchless sculptor dream,
Firm set in stone !   Down shaft and capital !
    When tides are full, what boots to dam the stream ?
What profits skill, in scale with miser gain ?
While greed triumphant, beauty pleads in vain.

The lad went on, and o'er, by Harold's bridge,
    The limpid stream that placid flowed around
The meads unmoved by ruin.   Slow the sedge
    Waved restless in the wind.   The snakeweed wound
Its slimy folds.   The broad-ribbed arch beheld
Its shade within the water as of eld.

Beyond, deep set within the minster wall,
   There stood unlatched a broad and studded gate;
Thence bordered paths, o'erhung with bushes tall,
   Went in and out the pleasaunce desolate ;
Untended now, all in disorder lay,
Unkempt the lawn, untrimmed the border bay.

The Provence rose for lack of trainer hand
   Ungraceful drooped ; the snow-flecked jessamine
In tangling clusters hung ; her chaliced wand
   Queen lily lifted doubtful ; bindweed twine
Ran over all unchecked; while pansies mild,
By ruder growth obscured, dejected smiled.

Above a porch, deep carved within the grit
   A pedant monk belaboured cogging boys,
With ' Disce, doce, aut discede ' writ
   Beneath for legend.   Often simple joys
Refreshen skill, and thus in sportive vein
The sculptor monk entabled learning's pain.

Alas for pity !   Windows wrecked and bare,
   Walls grimed by fierce explosive, since no force
Of sinewy arm or iron sledge could tear
   The bonded mass asunder, or the course
Of ruin run till fiery flame had set
Its scathing seal on wall and parapet.

4

Ah me ! How oft at foot of teacher monk
   The youngling here had hearkened legend old
Of saint or martyr, while weak childhood shrunk
   Aghast from tale of horror, trembling told
By some, ordained themselves ere long to know
Attaint of ill and chastening of woe !

Nor seldom, too, would Abbot Robert come
   Among them gracious, with uplifted hand
Bestowing blessing, while all knelt, and some,
   Thereafter bold, oft-granted boon demand
Of grace from task, with leave awhile to rove
Through garden, maze, or nearer woodland grove.

So nevermore ! Yet as he stood there rang
   Serene and clear the soft-toned sanctus-bell.
He started, doubtful. Whence the silenced clang
   That filled his ear, like throb of funeral knell?
What impious hand dare mime at awful cost
The solemn lifting of the atoning Host ?

The choir indeed was but a wreck—the roof
   Agape and robbed of rafter, joist, and lead;
Yet worse within, where pillaged tombs gave proof
   How sharp-set greed could spoil the very dead,
And Christian nobles scatter saintly bones,
And grope for gold in graves and charnel stones.

Amid the wreck a workman stood and tolled
   For sport the bell, while others jested nigh.
By righteous rage inspired, of horror bold,
   The lad stood forth, with loud and wrathful cry :
'What do ye, madmen ? Doubly mad to tempt
Your outraged God to visit base contempt !'

They drave him thence with laughter, floutings, blows.
   ' 'Tis but the shavelings' minion come again.
Goodlack ! how loud the monken fledgling crows,
   The oldsters gone from out their goodly den !'
So laughed they, scornful, mating evil speech
With stripes from aught that lay to hand or reach.

With bursting heart the lad escaped beyond
   The convent precincts. In the hither mead
He threw him down against the Lenten pond,
   Whose finny tenants, wont to welcome tread
And call, drew near, but rose and plashed in vain ;
The hands that fed should feed them ne'er again.

There lay the lad devoured by bitter thought,
   Till in his dream there mingled chiding voice,
Whose tones were music, sweet as lark's untaught
   Of bars and cage, whose gladsome notes rejoice
The wayworn trav'ler, lonely, longing sore
For joys of home, scarce counted joys before.

Beside the boy there knelt a maiden, meet
   For poet's song or painter's mimic pen,
Full like the lad that grovelled at her feet;
   But older, fairer, lovely queen of men;
Like Francis crowned with chevelure of gold,
That falling met her kirtle's swelling fold.

And 'Francis, cease, dear brother, cease to grieve,'
   She gently said, and kissed his angry brow;
·' 'Tis idle sorrow,—when comes ne'er reprieve,
   All things to storm do wisely bend and bow.
The king himself decreed the thing should be;
Who, then, can thwart or let his high decree?'

'The king!' he cried in angry scorn; 'his King
   Decrees him traitor to his kingly trust.
Last night, in dream, I saw an angel wing
   His way to earth, while abject in the dust
Lay king and council. Down they grovelling fell
Abashed—aghast as fiends at holy spell.'

'Hush, hush, dear Francis! Did knee-crooking knave
   But hear your madness, we were both undone.
Recall the reed that Abbot Robert gave
   Us both at parting. Patient hope in One,
In whom all things do centre, right or wrong;
By whom wax warriors weak, and striplings strong.'

' And striplings strong !' the lad exclaimed ; ' would I
   Were man to meet him in his royal place—
Foretell his fate, as when I saw him lie
   All terror-struck before the archangel's face ;
Denounce his crimes——' But here a stern voice bade
The boy be silent, and alarmed the maid,

Who rose dismayed.   Against a neighbouring tree
   He frowning stood, whose aspect chilled her blood.
Appalled she knelt, and whispering, ' It is he !'
   Embraced her brother.   ' Now, by holy rood,
No help have we, dear lad, but in the Lord—
The king himself has heard our every word !'

The boy sprang up with flashing eye, but all
   His courage failed in face of tiger wrath.
So torrent flood and noisy mountain fall
   Are lost in sea.   Across the grassy path
The despot strode, his cruel face aflame,
And bade the boy declare his place and name.

But he was silent, fear, with rage at fear,
   Restraining speech.   Again the tyrant cried,
The while his minions noiseless gathered near.
   Ungentle they, nor slow to serve his pride,
Yet some were moved to pity, when the maid
A sheltering clasp about her brother laid.

And meaning looks they cast. Too sweet and fair
   Was she by far to meet the greedy look
Of him who yet was never known to spare
   Or maid or wife; whose pride could never brook
Resistance in a subject; whose fell mocd,
Once roused, was ne'er abated but with blood.

Now outspake one, yet careful : ' These, my lord,
   Are gentle children, but betimes the boy
Is sprite-possessed. They dwell against the ford;
   Your highness may remember old Mountjoy
There pulled down quarry yester-eve. 'Tis said
There's fairy seal upon the youngster's head.'

' So ! Is it so ?' the king replied, his brow
   Relaxing at the fable. ' By the Mass !
The wench is comely. Let the losel go.
   Nay, now, good Denny; I would speak the lass.
Soft there, my sweeting, leave yon lout awhile ;
The king, methinks, may claim of right a smile.'

Our lord the king ! what subject dare gainsay
   His word or will ? Her angel face she raised
With pleading look, her bosom's trem'lous play
   Betraying fear. With greedy eye he gazed
Again and yet again, while plain to view
Unhallowed longing in his gazing grew.

Beneath his look she trembled like to fawn
   Wolf-charmed, that fears, yet harmless knows not why
Or what the danger, all its nature drawn
   To instinct dread. So looked she modest, shy,
Her soft eyes full of mild entreaty, while
His answered madly, full of pride and guile :

'So ! that is better. Sooth, I never knew
   Our Waltham woods contained such goodly deer ;
His chase in sight, the hunter must pursue.
   Sweet wench, a kiss. Nay, ne'er show sluttish fear.
Well, hark away, chaste quarry, yet that lip,
So ruddy ripe, enticeth lover sip.'

He now made sign that spake the king ; the maid
   With low obeisance quickly drew aside,
And with her drew her brother, as afraid
   He yet might wake the vengeful tyrant's pride ;
With evil smile the king beheld them go,
Then strode away with dark and knitted brow.

III.

Within the wood, removed a little way
   From town and convent, nigh a saucy brook
That, dancing into being, laughed at day,
   And joyous fled by thymy knoll and nook,
There stood a grange, age-bowed, with girdling stream
That flowed around with dark and sullen gleam.

Yet lilies grew, and spread within the pool,
    Their snow cups floating large amid their leaves ;
And mouse-ear near the bank, with parsley fool ;
    And loosestrife tall, with gladwyn's golden sheaves,
And mint that matted all the bank ; and weed
Obscure a host, that gained but little heed.

And over all a bridge with massy piers,
    And slender arch scarce lift above the moat
In lieu of drawbridge, long removed, that years
    Of peace made irksome. Nigh the bridge a boat
That floated idly where the lilies lay,
And in it Lilian, pure and chaste as they.

Her little hands, among the snow cups set,
    Drew slowly to her side the blossoms fair ;
Some few she chose by way of coronet,
    First kissed, then wound the wildings in her hair,
Her fair face kindling, and her azure eyes,
Love's mirrors, full of tender sympathies.

And ' Holy Mary, how the world is bright !'
    She thoughtful said ; ' what love her blessed Son
Must carry earth, to fashion such delight
    For careless eyes and hearts so hardly won !
I' faith, sith earth doth show such braggart wise,
How wondrous fair His own bright paradise !'

Through forest rift the sun, with ruddy glare,
  Shone full and low ; it kissed her virgin cheek
To summer glow, and dyed her glossy hair
  To deeper gold. No longer maiden meek,
But vestal priestess, robed with hallowing flame,
She seemed, and pure beyond attaint of shame.

So he confessed that stood beside the stream
  With clouded brow, and marked her guileless play
With leaf and lily. Not yet maiden dream
  Of love indulged, with mild complaisant sway
O'er manly hearts ; each impulse of her breast
Calm, chaste, and clear as babe's in cratchet nest.

'Twas he who friended Francis other while.
  Now stepping forth, he called the girl by name ;
She startling heard, then turned with sunny smile
  Her glowing face that way the summons came,
And merry laughed : 'Sir godsire, will you wear
My badge to-day, a lily light as air ?'

A bloom she plucked, and cast it lightly o'er
  The wat'ry marge ; he raised it to his lips,
Then, as recalled to purpose pressing sore
  For quick solution, answered gravely, 'Quips
Are folly now, so, Lilian, lay them by.
When fowlers snare, the turtle needs must fly.

'Ay, cease to toy with simples! There is one,
　My child, would toy in otherwise with thee
'Tis deathly pastime, therefore get thee gone
　Ere night, and keep thee close at Nazing Lea!
Hist, girl, more near! This very night the king
Intends thee aught but harmless visiting.

'So get thee gone with Francis, ere the night
　Garbs evil thought with opportune of gloom.
But keep my counsel. Mine were sorry plight—
　Perchance unheaded shoulders, bloody tomb—
Did Henry wot I sped forestalling bolt,
And warned his quarry out of Waltham holt!'

So whispered he. With shame and fear she heard,
　Yet nothing answered; only in her eyes
He read resolve, that needed never word
　For full expression—steadfast will that dies
Alone with dying. Never tyrant's slave
Were Lilian Lane, while earth had stainless grave.

'Bestir thee, Lilian! Show thy father's child!
　Ill fell the hap that took him yestermorn
To shire assize, yet worse that I beguiled
　The king to linger. Never's rose but thorn!
Would God the manor lay beneath the sea,
Ere harm, dear heart, should light on thee by me!

' And now farewell ! Keep close ! The danger past,
  I'll send thee word when thou mayst safe return.'
He kissed her cheek, she faintly smiled ; at last
  Came faltering speech : ' Fear not, good friend, I
    spurn
Unholy wooing ! Yet 'twere best to flee
Unharmed, than prove King Henry's courtesy.'

Her godsire gone, she hastened in, and soon
  Prepared for flight, stood eager by the gate ;
Why came not Francis ? He at close of noon
  Had sought the woodland. Now 'twas growing late,
The western sky o'erspread with crimson light,
And purple eve forerunning sable night.

She waited long, her breast aglow with shame,
  Her heart fast beating, while encroaching fear
Thrilled every nerve. Would God that Francis came !
  Now Hesper flamed, and danger drawing near
Tongued every leaf, and voiced each brook and rill
To wake in her, sweet child ! responsive thrill.

Made bold of gloom, the owl with dismal hoot
  Alarmed the wood ; the night-hawk weirdly chirred ;
From out the pool, disturbed, the timid coot
  Flew darkling upward. Sure the forest stirred
With step of stranger ! Cold and pale of fright,
She, trembling, fled for refuge in the night.

Unfollowed, soon her courage came again ;
  'Twas like that Francis loitered by the brook
That lapped the minster.   Now a laden wain
  Slow creaking by, she, grateful, comfort took
From honest presence; close within the sound
She kept, yet fearful, often gazing round.

The convent wall now rose to view.   She sighed :
  ' Alas ! were Abbot Robert but within,
How gladly would the holy father hide
  His whilom charge from pursuance of sin !
Distressful change !   Now royal might is right ;
No convent aid awaits unhappy wight !'

No sound arose but distant roister shout
  From roadside inn or township hostelry,
With swir of ash that lithely tossed about
  Its yellowing tufts in aimless revelry.
Not far away the ruined minster stood—
Dark, lifeless, dull, fit home for ghostly brood.

With hasty hand she made the holy sign
  On breast and brow, then stealthy made her way
Toward the ruins.   Shapes unseen, benign,
  Guard now her harmless footsteps.   Sanct array
Befriend her, helpless !   Hark ! what descant rude
Assails her ear, and shocks night's solitude ?

See, torches flame! Amid their yellow glare
  There treads the causey merry-making crew ;
And in their midst—alas! what did he there?—
  Her brother guarded! Spellbound, full in view
She stood, nor further thought of self or flight,
In fear for him and his untoward plight.

Too soon perceived of all, loud laughter broke
  Anew the night. Then over all a cry
Rang sharply out, and Francis wildly spoke :
  'Fly, Lilian, fly! Think not of me, but fly !
There's harm against thee.' Fearless as to cost,
Thus much he cried, with more in clamour lost.

Now came the king, and did the trembling maid
  Half mocking reverence—'Marry, then, fair quest,
You save some seeking.' So he blandly said
  With careless smile, then haughty bade the rest
Halt by the stream, which done, a space apart
He drew the maid, with base and villain heart,

And sought to kiss her lips. But with a cry
  She brake away, through grant of helpful strength
From angel guard. Enraged he saw her fly
  Tow'rds Harold's bridge, and followed scarce a length
Behind ; but fleet as startled bird on wing
Of fear she fled, and soon outran the king.

She gained the bridge, but looking back to know
    Herself escaped, her foot slipped and she fell.
By dread aroused, though blinded with the blow,
    She stagg'ring rose. Ah me ! what tongue shall tell
The power that led the fainting girl so near
The starlit stream that washed the flinty pier.

Again a fall—a cry—the waters close,
    And, weirdly murmuring, tell no further tale ;
But, horror-stricken, well the tyrant knows
    What bleeding lies beneath their gleamy veil.
' Ho ! lights and men ! Quick, knaves ! your heads shall
      pay
For laggard help or ill-conceived delay.'

They drew her forth—a lily on her brow,
    Self-twined. Sweet Lilian, loveliest flower of all,
Her tresses dank and tangled, living glow
    Gone evermore ! Ah, sad yet welcome pall !
And stream more kind than stony heart, that bade
Death's gate unbar to shield the gentle maid.

IV.

Escaped, the stag regains the thorny brake,
    And panting lies, concealed in ferny bed ;
The hounds, athirst, their baffled fever slake
    At rushy spring ; the jaded hunters spread
Their evening meal, with glaive and staff and horn
Laid idle by at foot of beech and thorn.

Alone, apart, from ardour of the chase,
   From hounds and men, the king at length drew rein
Beside an oak of mighty growth, whose base
   Usurped the hill, and overeyed the plain,
Where, red-roofed, dim, 'neath evening's purple crown,
Mid stream and tree, reposed the quiet town.

He wound his horn, but scarce the cheerful call
   Had roused the woodland echoes out of sleep,
To make reply all dreamily, and fall
   Again to rest, than out the welkin steep
Fierce lightning leaping, cleft low-hanging cloud,
And shook the holt with thundering long and loud.

'Twas lightning such the wood was all ablaze
   With flood of fire, and murmuring shrank from flame
That living leaped.   Earth plainly shook.   By craze
   Of terror moved, one wildly loud acclaim
Uprose from bird and beast, then silence fell
Profound as death o'er plain and crest and dell.

Again the bolt leaped out its lurid crown,
   And scarce the king could curb his steed for awe.
Heart smitten now, a neighbouring oak came down
   With rend and rush and crash that shook the shaw;
Supreme in ruin as in girth profound,
The falling monarch spread destruction round.

The king's gaze set upon the tree, there came
　　Unseen a youth from out the nearer wood.
'Twas Francis, madness in his look, and flame
　　Of frenzy in his bearing.　Full he stood
Before the king, and fearless bade him hear
Malefic doom and retribute severe.

'Accurst of all, and callous as the sea,
　　That aye devours and yet is never full ;
And never worn of wanton cruelty,
　　But brooding ill while waves and winds are dull ;
Here would I slay thee, strong in righteous hate,
Did not thy God decree severer fate.

'So live thou on, earth's malison !　Fulfil
　　Thy course unclean, like pestilential star
That banes in flight, and, failing, darkens still
　　Men's lives in dying.　Tyrant ! better far
Thy bloody axe and dungeon grave forlorn,
Than lifelong hate and unborn ages' scorn.

'Ay, frown at will !　Hark yonder thunder roll,
　　That shuddering earth repeats in hollow tone !
Thou know'st it well, for, monster, in thy soul
　　Thou hear'st again thine ordnance' murd'rous groan
That told thee Boleyn died, her guiltless head
Laid low to smooth adult'rous bridal bed !

'Mark, too, yon flame, o'erleaping Waltham tower,
  Where, snatched from thee, thy latest victim lies.
All powerful thou, and soulless in thy power,
  What friend but death dare thwart thy tyrannies?
Thine, tyrant, thine, to bid sweet Lilian die;
Thine, fiend, the curse that fired her glazing eye!

'Fulfil thy fate, thou scourge of earth and bane
  Of all things good. In lust and blood and crime
Fulfil it; then find Herod's doom. Attain
  To death in life; and, noisome in thy prime,
Call death in vain, while demons shrink aghast
To know hell pain by mortal pang surpast.

'Then die to glad thy people by thy death,
  And lift a load from off a nation's heart,
Thy name recalled with loathing, bated breath,
  And curse in utterance. Tyrant, thine the part
To show that earth can rival hell in ill,
And demons vile, yet kings be viler still.'

The lightning sprang, the thunder shook the roof
  Of listening heaven. The lad with gesture wild
Exulted loudly: 'Murd'rer! 'tis approof
  Of Lilian's curse. Now live, thy soul beguiled
From ill to ill, till, all thy crimes complete,
  Thou goest hence to retribution meet.'

He turned and fled. The tyrant, sore amazed,
  Nor sought nor thought to intercept his flight,
But haggard smiled. ' In sooth the lout is crazed !'
  He muttered fearful, then from lowering night
And fury-storm turned homeward, evermore
His stricken soul a prey to torments sore.

*   *   *   *   *

Beyond the sea in quiet cloister fane,
  Unhavocked yet by royal spoilers' hand,
A little while there lingered Francis Lane,
  To die ere manhood, far from home and land.
Too large his heart to bear life's sterner cross
Of blighted hopes, sharp grief, and bitter loss.

Soon Abbot Fuller died, his convent home
  Become a mine whence all men quarried stones ;
Contented still through faith in Him whence come
  Both good and ill, he calmly slept, his bones
Laid reverent to their rest, where priests still lift
To prayerful lips love's last benignant gift.

But oft of night within the chapel old—
  Our Lady's, spoiled of all its ancient show—
A tonsured priest and lad with locks of gold
  Are seen absorbed in converse sad and low,
While dirge-like, soft, unearthly numbers rise,
And fill the church with wailful symphonies.

And Lilian Lane beside the murmuring stream
   Is seen full oft when stars give misty light,
And mead and tree show ghostly in the gleam
   The crescent moon affords the new-throned Night—
To Harold's bridge will come, then fearful look
In haste behind, and vanish in the brook.

And still at night, when winter blast and gale
   Entice to warmth within the hostel's glow,
The din of song and laughter hushed, the tale
   Of Lilian sweet is told in accents low ;
While honest rage each rustic bosom fires
To scorn of greed and hate of base desires.

PLEASURES.

A ROOM full of books, and a bickering fire,
   Rain on the pane, and the wuthering gale,
Turbulent, petulant, twisting the briar,
   Bowing the willows and shaking the pale.
Sweet ! But my spirit is aching for more,
A face at my knee that is gone evermore.

A song that is sweet and a tale that is told
   Breathless in gloom that is eerie with blaze ;
A strain that is struck from a harpsichord old,
   Whirling of maidens in waltz and in maze.
Sweet ! But my spirit is aching for more,
A voice that by me shall be heard nevermore.

Tossing of bumper and kissing of cup,
    Wine that is ruddy, or yellow as gold ;
Wit that is spiteless, though wassailers sup,
    Laughter invading Care's innermost hold.
Sweet ! But my spirit is aching for more,
A kiss from the lips that shall kiss nevermore.

A walk through a wood in the twilight, or glen
    Eglantine sweet, that is honeyed as breath
Of paradise, open a moment that men
    May mock at Life's phantom, impassionless Death.
Sweet ! But my spirit is aching for more,
A comrade whose converse is lost evermore.

A grave in God's acre, 'neath cypress and yew,
    Apart from the pompous, the wealthy, and proud ;
Restful for ever 'neath daisy and dew,
    Happy befreed from intolerant crowd.
Sweet ! Ah, but sweeter my bliss evermore,
Asleep with my sweeting to wake nevermore.

REVERIE.

THOUGHTFUL seated at my casement,
    All the world beside asleep ;
Placid Night her courtier phalanx
    Radiant leading out the deep.
Many things I thought, but chiefly,
    Mystery of mysteries—Life !
All its chances, all its changes ;
    All its failures, all its strife.

Strife of Wealth with wan-cheeked Labour,
 Olive Peace with warrior wreath ;
Vice and Shame with stern-faced Virtue,
 Med'cine, Christlike, grappling Death ;
Mis'ry matched with wasteful splendour,
 Poverty agrip with Greed ;
Love with Hate, content with Envy,
 Callous Gain with griping Need.

Sudden woke the wind, and, fresh'ning,
 Shook the woodland, till its roar
Filled the air, like ocean breaking
 Rageful o'er rock-bonded shore ;
And within my soul there sounded,
 Loud and clear as clarion call,
Echo-answer to the problem,
 Holding mind and thought in thrall :

Ye, ye there ! ye that press a gilded throne,
 And proudly view from far your people's state ;
Too high uplift to hear their often moan,
 'To catch their curse, or harrowing scowl of hate ;
Who, flatt'ry-fed, persuade yourselves that ye
Are gods, and godlike, lords of destiny :
  The glass is turned, its sands are well-nigh run—
  Grains, grains, a grain, and all your day is done !

Ye, ye there ! ye that crowd about the stool
 Of purpled clown or tyrant—meanly met
To cringe and fawn, or be he knave or fool ;
 To play the part of pander ; eager set

To varnish shame, to pamper pride and lust—
Intemp'rate all to hail him wise and just :
    The glass is turned, its sands are well-nigh run —
    Grains, grains, a grain, and all your day is done !

Ye, ye there ! ye fine-linened, at your ease,
    That delicately fare from day to day ;
Who compass earth yourselves alone to please,
    Nor care who else shall fall beside the way ;
Fast harnessed to your car, so ye may glide,
Unvexed adown—to ye—Life's crimson tide :
    The glass is turned, its sands are well-nigh run—
    Grains, grains, a grain, and all your day is done !

Ye, ye there ! ye that grind the helpless poor,
    And sweat and starve your brethren ; in the mire
Your sisters trampling, so your warehouse floor
    May higher heap—what matter though they hire
Their bodies out for bread ? Your daughters grow
The richer for their mis'ry, shame, and woe :
    The glass is turned, its sands are well-nigh run—
    Grains, grains, a grain, and all your day is done !

Ye, ye there ! ye that live to toil, and pray
    For death, whose lives are less than that of beast ;
Death-weary ye that chide slow Night's delay,
    And sighing see the gilding of the east ;
Whose loftiest hope, whose dream, whose heav'n, is rest ;
That but attained, oh how supremely blest !
    The glass is turned, its sands are well-nigh run—
    Grains, grains, a grain, and all your toil is done !

Ye, ye there ! ye whose coward spirits quail
  At thunder-clap of evil or annoy ;
Who dare no hero deed, who craven fail
  At trumpet-call of duty, wide the buoy
Of danger steering—up ye, up and do
Your part in earth's stern warfare ! Up ! or rue
    The turning of the glass. Its sandlets run
    Swift, swift, and swift ! Full soon your day is done !

Ye, ye there ! ye whose lofty souls are set
  To crusade right—Godlike to battle wrong ;
Who sternly smite at ill wherever met,
  And traverse life triumphant, zealous, strong—
Your warrior course a beacon blazing high,
That craft and greed and lust abhorrent fly :
    No glass ye need, for you no sandlets run—
    Earth, heav'n, or heav'ns, your day is never done !

Ye, ye there ! ye whose flashing pinions fright
  The shrinking sky, as lightning-winged ye speed,
With captain message from the Lord of light
  To them that wage life's warfare—be their creed
Whate'er it may—so but they wrestle on,
Stout-souled till all the fight be fought and won :
    Speed forth, speed forth, ye helpful host, and bring
    Love, love, and love, upon your ardent wing !

THE NAIL.

I.

JESSAMINE, jessamine, sparkling with dew,
That clingeth my casement and peepeth athrough,
 Say not what thou seest, I pray—
If kisses a score on his picture I set,
Or nightly my pillow with pearly tears wet,
 My sweetheart so far, far away !

Gillyflower, gillyflower, yellow as gold,
Wall-sentinel hardy, and watchful, and bold,
 That challengest tempest and gale,
Bid now the breeze tarry and question him straight,
Where lingers my lover, such long time belate ?
 What hinders his home-turning sail ?

Rosemary, rosemary, on to his breast
A spriglet I fastened, first kissed and carest,
 For surer remembrance and stay !
Say, has he forgotten ?   Ah me ! can it be
That seamen are fickle as ocean and sea,
 Unfaithful as billow and spray ?

Thus Hester Turvil, while with careful hand
She twined the lissom jasmine's sinuous spray
About her lattice.   Bright the morn, and bland
The summer breeze while scent of upturned hay

Or sweltering cock came o'er the Redriff mead.
The girl was fair, with eyes of honest gray,
That, questioned, answered, fearless ; hair that spread
Unhindered down her cheek and neck, and lay
Curled on her bosom like to babe asleep.
Wide open was the casement, and her face
Was all to view, with borderage of deep
And glossy green, that, as it would embrace
Her beauty, bent now here and there adown ;
While pendent o'er her head a milky way
Of star-white blossoms made befitting crown,
For maiden pure as Dian's famed array.

The house was small, but set in larger ground
That verged upon the down—not yet a name,
But ample, breezy.   Past its northern bound,
Thames calmly flowing by was all aflame
With kiss of Phœbus.   Slowly down the stream
A privateer swept graceful.   On her mast,
High perched, o'er sail, and yard, and stay supreme,
A shipman waved adieu ; while half aghast,
Half proud, his sweetheart stood upon the bank,
And, tearful, shook her kerchief in reply.
Now music brake upon her deck.   Down sank
Fair Hester's hands ; her heart with heavy sigh
Swelled as she gazed, and fell and swelled again,
As tear on tear bedewed the lattice sill.
' So parted we !   How long it seems !   The pain
Aye wakes within me, spite of pride and will,

Whene'er each goodly vessel, venture rife,
Glides down to dare the hazard of the sea,
With added foeman's hate—to wail of wife,
Or heart-broke sweetheart's keener misery !

' Raleigh could home, and home to cruel doom !
And he could come, how canst thou still delay?
What spell so lurks in horrid ordnance boom,
Or clash of steel on biter-steel, to sway
Beyond the charm of home, or wife, or love ?
Why didst thou leave me ?—what and thou wert poor !
Enough was mine to lift us far above
The need to scrape, or shut unkindly door
On hungry wand'rer !'
                          So the maiden sighed,
And all her gaze upon the river gleam,
And ship, slow-moving o'er opposing tide,
Down to the hapful ocean's broader stream—
Knew not herself observed until a voice
Manly and pleasant brake upon her ear.
' Good-morrow, Mistress Hester ! other choice
I had not than to seek the garden rear.
So long I rapped unheeded at the door !'
Out of her dream awaked, the maid looked down,
Then courteous : ' Good-morrow, Master Moore,'
Made answer, yet with shadow of a frown
Upon her face, like cloud at eve, awhile
Dimming the brow of Cynthia, but to melt
Erelong within the virgin goddess' smile.
Thus on the maiden's brow the shadow dwelt
An instant and was gone.

'I'll come anon,'
She added smiling, as she did repent
Her first vexation. Yet again, where shone
The moving ship, a wistful look she bent
While gently drawing to the latticed pane,
Then snail-paced came to greet unwelcome guest—
Unwelcome most of all as would-be swain,
Importunate in parley as in quest.

Her parents dead, the maiden dwelt alone—
Her only brother erewhile drowned at sea—
With sturdy Hal the gardener, and Joan
His wife, for housely guard and company.
Well dowered beyond the hazard of her birth,
Her gold attracted some, yet more herself;
Her beauty justly held of greater worth,
With virtue than her store of meaner wealth.
Of these was Moore the stapler ; well-to-do
Himself, she knew him honest in his suit ;
A proper man withal, complacent, too,
In speech, if proud as ran the common bruit.

His suit she had refused, for Richard Gray
Had won her heart ; and who could blame the maid ?
Tall was the youth, with frame compact, where lay
Strength without tyranny ; and eyes, where played
God's light of truth incessant ; lips that smiled
But seldom, and the most part firm comprest,
Gave pledge of resolution, and beguiled
The more by smiling—like to dewy crest

Of rose, that, wooed to opening by the ray,
Unveils her virgin glories, trembling oft
At kiss of beam and all unusèd play
Of breeze amid her blushing petals soft.

But Gray was poor.   Long time he silence kept
While many a meaner urged less truthful tale ;
Till one day, playful chidden, ardour swept
Away restraint, like leaves in autumn gale,
And burning lips spake burning words that shook
His soul in utterance.

               Naught did Hester speak,
But tremulous smiled with shy and tearful look ;
Which seen, he snatched her to his breast—her cheek,
Her hair, her lips, with kisses overstrewn.
' Sweet love, sweet love, long time I held aloof !'
He whispered after, rapture sober grown.
' None loving, sure, as I, for fear reproof,
As being poor, should shame me, did I dare
Lift lover eyes to beauty rightly dowered !
Nor dared I now, perchance, but that I fare
To-morrow to the main, with Master Howard,
Who joins ship with Sir Walter !'

                    Hester here
Made mild remonstrance : ' Richard, sweetheart, nay,
You must not go.   'Twere coward part to fear
What jealous tongues, of envy barbed, may say !'
But Gray was firm.   ' I may not wed you, sweet,
Till first I prove what Fortune has in store
For noble leaders and a gallant fleet
On famed Guiana's wild but golden shore !'

And so they parted. When the fleet returned,
Gray came not, but, as rumour ran, had gone—
With others, who the thought of home had spurned
Till wealth was theirs—in one small bark alone
Far south, resolved to prove the Spanish main.
This told to Hester, first vexation filled
The maiden's breast ; till love erelong with pain
And pride at war, full soon resentment stilled.
The matter known to Moore, again his suit
He eager pleaded ; would not take gainsay,
Intent to prove the saw, ' Love's golden fruit
He plucks that's present; failure waits delay.'
Yet made he never progress. Full a year
Close siege he laid, but Hester aye withstood
Siege and pursuit. Yet did he persevere,
Resolved to win her or by ill or good.

So came he now, all overjoyed,—for news
Had reached him of Gray's death—but seemly yet,
And grave of aspect, like to him that views
Another's grief with semblance of regret.
And, ' Mistress Hester,' slowly he began,
With feigned reluctance, ' yester eve there came
Two seamen hither.—Yet 'twere better plan
Yourself did hear their tale. They name a name
And matter such I dare not speak. Too well
Indeed I love, by word or look to wound.'
So said he crafty, pausing oft to swell
His words' importance. From her lips no sound
Came forth, though thrice they parted ; but her eyes

Spake deadly fear, with cheek that blanched—outdid
The jessamine for paleness.　Soon, surprise
O'ercome, and sense of fallen evil chid,
She spake him coldly : ' I will see the men,
E'en as you wish, if you will comrade them.'
He gone with show of sorrow, woke again
The love-pang in her soul.　Like lily stem,
Worm-furrowed, drooped she o'er the garden-bed,
Dismayed, and trembling oft with unknown fears.
Unheeded all, the cosset pansies spread
Their velvet pates ; she saw them not for tears.
Unconscious plucked, all vainly poured the clove
His breeze-enriching perfume ; unheard hummed
The bee o'er bloom ; unheard in lilac grove
The linnet cheerful sang.　Her heart, benumbed
With prescience of evil, took no heed
Of song, or scent, or beauty.
　　　　　　　　　　　　'Gainst the wall
An arbour stood with bindweed canopied,
Whose chaliced blooms, heat-sweltered, 'gan to fall
In pride, and close their all too fragile bells.
Here Hester now retired, and sat her down
At sound of nearing footsteps.　Sudden swells
Her bosom as 'twould rend its gaoler gown.
She, shivering, sighed.　But now the shipmen nigh,
Too proud the common herd should mark her pain,
She rose to meet them, making fit reply
To courteous salutation, yet was fain
To claim the latticed arbour's friendly aid ;
Her little hand amid the trailing green
Hid where it clasped.

Their court'sies o'er, these made
A pause as doubtful, till with steady mien
She bade them venture freely on their tale.
Then one began, not seldom to his mate
Turning for confirmation : ' Fray and gale
Had hindered so their project, 'twas but late
They made for England.   Then at Plymouth stayed
Some while ere coasting up to London town.
Ill news they bore, and therefore had delayed
The telling of set purpose.   Now adown
The river sailing with the eventide,
On other venture bent, they gathered heart
To tell the tale, they might not longer hide,
Of honour, since so soon they must depart.'

This given—with often garnishing of oath—
The mariner revealed how they and Gray
Had shipmates been, and afterward how both
Had fought beside him in a Spanish fray ;
Had seen him fall, and drawn him out the throng,
To know him smitten, and to death, by ball
From arquebuse.   Here paused the sailor long
At sob from Hester, overcome, for all
Her will to conquer poignancy of loss.
Now Moore came forward : ' Hester, dearest, bear
The tidings like yourself; 'tis bitter cross :
Would I could bear it wholly, or might share !'
So said he softly, taking in his own
The little hand that cold as winter lay
Passive within his grasp.   A sigh, a moan,
And now again herself.   ' Now say your say,
Good friend, and quickly.'

'Nay, there's little more,'
The man rejoined ; ' he lies in shade of rock,
But this we took from off his neck. He wore
It aye as philtre. 'Tis a scissored lock
Of hair, sweet mistress.'
From his outstretched hand
She trembling took a dingy parchment twirl ;
Which, slowly freed from circling silken band,
Revealed, safe kept, a soft and glossy curl.

'Twas all he had to tell. A piece of gold
She gave him for a largess, and beside
For unkind tidings, not unkindly told,
A word or two of thanks ; then, downcast, hied
The house within to gratify her grief.
The seamen now retiring, further gift
Moore made them after converse low and brief—
Well pleased, th' event so fair for lover drift.

*   *   *   *   *

Her own love-pledge ! Now died within her soul
Doubting and hope. Long time with burning eyes
She gazed upon the ringlet, pearly dole
Of greeting falling as from April skies.
Such cruel ending to her dream ! Sweet maid,
The livelong day she dwelled upon the pledge,
Low sighing like to gust in summer glade,
Or breeze of autumn midst the dirgeful sedge.

*   *   *   *   *

II.

A year was gone. Amid her shrubs and flowers
Sweet Hester Turvil sat. Physician Time,
All-healing leech, had charged the passing hours
With med'cine meet for heart-ache. Now the chime
That, breaking out St. Olaf's tower, along
The down swept joyous, waking all the bells
Of hollyhock and lily into song,
No longer jarred on sorrow. Softly swells
Her breast; she lists the merry clangour; drinks
The harmony of bell, and breeze, and leaf
With kindling eye and heart. Not seldom thinks
She still of Gray; too deep her love for grief
To be but matter of an idle day,
Or easy laid aside, like winter glove,
At beam of spring or summer's early ray—
Far otherwise did Hester Turvil love.

E'en now her thoughts were with him. Did he share
In his new home unchangeful, aught that woke
Within her thrill of pleasure? More, could care,
Or aught that stirred life's lesser life, invoke
His soul to sympathy with earth and her?
Thus Hester, pensive, while the summer gale,
Made bold of beauty, harmless paramour,
Played with her curls and kissed her forehead pale.

A nearing footstep chasing thought, she turned
Her lovely head. 'Twas Moore. With quick'ning stride
And flashing eye, and cheek that ruddy burned,
He drew anear and sat him by her side.

6

Persistent suitor through another year,
To him an age, he had been yet content,
Were he but in her thought, to prove and bear
Her every whim and mood ; till, sorrow spent,
Pursuit so patient, constant, should prevail—
With aidance of maid instinct—once again
To waken virgin fancies.
               Such assail,
And subtle, aided by surcease of pain,
Began to tell, as sap and mine will fall
Full oft the fortress laughing storm to scorn.
Quick-eyed to see the change, more willing thrall
He showed than ever, till one lucky morn,
Not long agone, he won constrained consent
To plead, and soon thereafter ribbon pledge,
Part snatcht, part given !
               Returning Springtime lent
To lover fervour, fire ; and Summer, edge
Setting to passion, grew he resolute
To end and soon in all-forgetful flame
Of rapturous possession, endless suit.
And ' Hester, Hester, will you never name,'
He cried, his lover greeting scarcely o'er,
' The day to me as hither taste of heav'n ?
Was ever love as mine?   Could lover more
Than I, or give thee more than I have given
Of faithful service?   List the jocund bells,
How sweet they peal around !   Each merry tongue
To me seems loud with call to love, compels
My soul to madness !'

Thus he, while she hung
Her head irresolute, then, soft and low
As woodland whisper : ' Nay, far otherwise
The music speaks to me. 'Twas even now
The thought arose—Can earth to Paradise
Fond greeting send, or thrill in mortal breast
Touch kindred chord in heav'n-containèd ghost.'
Beyond him was the thought. His face confest
Perplexity and doubt. Then happy crost
His mind this thought, 'She thinks her still of Gray !'
So made her answer : ' All too great their joy,
Safe-havened souls, to share concern of clay,
Or otherwise their bliss would know alloy !
How oft we spurn a present happiness
For fancied future good ; or let the mind
Out ancient ill beget new bitterness,
Fortune anigh with kindly hand to bind
Our grief-wounds up, and, wise physician, pour
A double meed of balsam in the gape.
This known, bethink you, Hester, how much more
Of grief were theirs than happiness ! Escape
There could be none from sorrow !'

                  This he said,
Then crafty turned the thought another way,
A short time silent first, with down-bent head,
As one that deeply brooded. ' Yet there may
Be cognisance, for some do so maintain.
But if so, then how much the greater need
Of surveillance in us to spare them pain,
Who painless else would have us equal freed !
No marriage can be there ; but what hath earth

Of larger bliss than pact of man and maid
Constrained thereto of love? 'Tis said the birth
Of such is wrought in heaven by spirit aid.
I love you, Hester, dearly ; every thought
Bent to your worship ! Think you he you mourn
Would not the rather know you overfraught
With joy than still distressful and forlorn ?'
Much more he urged, with plaint, and sigh, and vow,
Till part o'erborne of vehemence, part won,
She answered as he wished. Who joyous now
As Moore, at last his weary suitage done ?

III.

Again a year, and Autumn 'gan to gild
The roadside maple and the o'erhanging elm ;
A plaintive song the restless robin trilled,
Fearful of sharp-fanged Winter, and the whelm
Of leafage ruin lurking in his train.
'Twas eve, but warm and calm, and Hester Moore
Sat with her babe, her pretty God-sent gain,
Beside an open window.
                            Slowly o'er
The grassy down eve's dusky phantoms spread
With shades amid the garden walks and trees.
Sweet was the air ; the dying leaves and dead
Sent up their damp cool fragrance. Scarce the breeze
Had strength to lift the lilac's thinning spray,
Or bear the garden odours out the pale.
Yet lingered in the west a golden ray,
Set in a field of purple. Eager tale

Of nearing night one bright star told.   The moon
Peeped out, and, peeping, sank her fretted horn
Amid the ruddy gloom.   Benignant boon
Of sleep—full oft to weary souls forlorn
Their one sad comfort, all beside denied—
Calm night began to proffer loving-kind.
And Hester, bending o'er her babe, to chide
Had thought, the boy to sleeplessness inclined ;
But chid the thought instead and brake in song,
As mothers oft in whom the angel gift
Of song lies dormant, unrevealed for long,
Till infants lisping at their ears they lift
Responsive music.
                    In the fading light
A lullaby of pensive note she sang,
Unheedful in her task of nearing wight,
And the returning gate's discordant clang.

LULLABY.

Sleep, darling, sleep ! the bright day draws to end,
And starry girdled Night on tiptoe stands.
Nay, baby, nay ! the shadows deepening blend,
'Tis time for sleep ; lift not those pretty hands
Up to thy mother's lips, but, nuzzling, rest
Thy harmless head against her sheltering breast !

Sleep, darling, sleep ! what, not enough of day
For babeling stranger, all so late come forth
World-bourne unknown, to join dull earth's array ?
Alas ! the venture was but little worth.
Come ! close those wondering eyes, the night is nigh ;
Sleep, sweet one, sleep to cratchet lullaby !

Sleep, darling, sleep ! ere long thou wilt be glad—
If so may be—to shut thy senses all
On garish earth's uneasy pleasures, clad
In bubble vesture, but the more to thrall ;
Wilt woo the sleep thou scornest now, to find
Sleep shun thee in her turn with vengeful mind !

Ere long upon her breast the youngling slept,
And Hester gently laid him in his nest,
Thrice kissed his dimpled hand, and noiseless crept
Away to close the casement.   In the west
Of purpled gold there yet remained a gleam,
Wherein outshone the amorous star of eve.
Her eyes drawn thither, sudden stifled scream
Brake from her fearful.   'Neath the casement eave
A man stood, mournful gazing.   God ! 'twas ghost
Of Gray !   Aghast she clutched the oaken sill
And frightened gazed, all power of movement lost
In stupefaction both of mind and will !
The figure moved, came nearer.   Then the voice
She loved so well spake sadly : ' Hester, sweet,
I am no spirit ! yet might well rejoice
To be fordone of Spaniard than to greet
My love, and find her lost to me for aye.'
Now came back knowledge, saddest gift of all,
To Hester, anguish stricken.   Sigh on sigh
Fled from her lips.   She trembled as to fall,
But brave through all her misery, fought away
Her untold sorrow, and her shivering hand
Held forth in swift entreaty.

' Richard Gray !
At home ! alive ! Not slain in foreign land !
My love ! my love ! Ah, God ! my heart will break ;
They told me you were dead.   Nay, brought me back
The curl I gave you, love, for love's sweet sake.
From off your neck they took it.'
                              ' Villains, black
And heartless, so to cozen trustful maid,'
Gray fiercely made reply.   ' Dear heart, I know
The whole vile story.   Sweet, you were betrayed
By him for whom you took the altar vow.'

Here Hester moaned in pain, her aching head
Laid low upon the sill.   ' The men were not
With me, nor in the venture.   That they said
Was false and planned by Moore—a crafty plot
To win you to his wooing ; 'twas confest
Awhile ago on deathbed by the man
That spake you.'
                    Thus asserting, Gray caressed
The sorrow-stricken head.   ' This much I can,
And may, my darling, ere I prove again
The sea, by far less treacherous and bare
Of charity than man.   Forget the pain
I bring you, Hester.   For your sake I spare
The villain that has robbed me of the prize
I covet more than all the hidden gold
Of great Montsuma.   Love, unclose those eyes ;
No thought of blame, but only love untold
For ever in my heart I bear thee still.'

So pleaded he, each soft and glossy curl
Kissing again and yet again, until
She lift her head to ease its giddy whirl
A moment on his breast.
                  But now a cry
Came from the crib.   She started back.   ' Ah me !
I am both wife and mother—dare not lie
On other breast than his, who—misery
Of miseries—in God's own house I swore
To love and honour.'   Here she bitter laughed,
Then cried : ' Oh, love, why cam'st thou not before,
Or why didst leave me ?   'Tis a deadly draught
For me, unfaithful; yet two years I fought
Against his persecution.   Richard, go ;
My heart is breaking.—Hush thee, babe ! 'tis naught,
Thy mother watches.   Mother !   Ah, the woe
Henceforth for me !
              Yet, Richard, go not yet ;
We ne'er must meet again.   This kiss and this,
Begging forgiveness, on thy lips I set,
With thousand tears for suppliants.   Set a kiss
In turn on mine, for sign thou dost forgive,
Then leave me and forget.'
                 ' Nay, Hester, nay !
I leave thee since I must, but while I live
Fond thought of thee shall gird my every way.
I live but loving thee.   God keep thee, sweet !
Be happy an thou canst.   This circlet twine
About thy bantling's neck, and should it meet
Thy husband's eye, then tell him 'tis for sign
Of peace between us for the sake of one

Dear to us both, but doubly dear to me.
This also, darling! Hester, I have done
The thing I sought to do—am rich ; the sea
Was mine of wealth to me and some few more,
Who scorned return to England as we came,
But snatched a bark and cruised the Spanish shore.
Thereafter aided by the lucky fame
That all the English were returned again,
All unexpected we, town after town
We took, and one rich galleon on the main
A storm had havocked.
             Ne'er did Fortune frown
Upon us till, returning South, a gale
Beat us for days within the peaceful sea.
So did we then as Drake, and carried sail
From isle to isle to Chaney. Thence came free
About the world, until old England's clift—
Hailed with a shout and burst of jovial din—
Gladdened our eyes like honest star in rift,
That helps lost trav'ler out of marshy gin.

'So am I rich, dear love, and should you need,
As yet you may—nay, heed me, sweet!—this ring
And letter shown to Master Silversteed,
The Turkey merchant of Old Change, will bring
Ungrudging help.'
             A little while they clung
Speechless, amid the deepening darkness, save
For sigh and kiss, until a ship-bell rung
Louder than common. Then, low-toned and grave,

Gray spake again : ' Farewell ! farewell ! the tide
Doth serve and I must go, for so I pledged
This morning, heart-sick of the world.   Abide
The sorrow, Hester, though 'tis dagger-edged.
The curl you gave me still is next my heart,
Dearer the gift than gem from Indian mine !
No matter where, each night I draw apart
And kiss the pledge and pray the blessed Nine
To guard the giver.'
                    Trembling all, ' Farewell !'
She sighed, as slow he drew from her embrace.
' Think of me sometimes.   Evermore will dwell
In me remembrance.'   Anguish in her face,
She watched him as he mournful trod the walk,
Heard the gate clang, beheld him wave adieu,
Then turned to mourn, like luce on broken stalk,
Above her babe, her heart rived through and through.

IV.

Again the belfry spake, but seldom stroke
And dull that smote the soul of her that hung
Above her coffined babe, and, wailing, broke
The lethal stillness, while she frantic clung—
A moment yet entreating—to the dead
That kindly neighbour hands must now remove.
'Twas Hester Moore, upon whose gentle head,
As unkind Fate would all its rigours prove,
Blow upon blow had fall'n in cruel wise.   ‚
First Moore began, passion at end, to show
Neglectful ; then, his treachery known, disguise

Threw off, and reckless frowned upon the woe
That paled his victim's face.
                            With proud restraint
Hester withheld reproach, nor ever word
Spake of her sorrow; neither sigh nor plaint
Making to friend or neighbour, though the sword
Of silence probed but deeper hopeless wound.
Nor this the whole.   Ere long another ill
Was added, when her girlhood's home she found
Sold to repair a traffic loss, with still
A debt behind.   'Twas fate, for hitherto
Moore had been prosperous in his ventures.   Now,
As Fortune did eschew him, daily grew
Matters to worse.   Ere long the Barley Mow
Knew him for often guest, since now he sought,
Madman, to drown the sting and sense of loss
In vinous revelry, oblivion, bought
With after pain, more poignant than the cross
Laid on him rightful.
                      Thus he grew to sot
Within a year.   And but a week agone,
Drunken returning home, from out its cot,
Deaf to entreaty, took his infant son.
At end his maudlin tenderness, again
Rejecting aid, he had the babe laid down,
But stumbled, and, unable to regain
Himself, had crushed the babe upon the stone—
The marble hearthstone, hateful evermore.
So died the boy.   To-day, to wakeless sleep,
They lay him where the river laps the shore,
Miming the surge sonore of mighty deep,

With laughing wavelets, children of the rill,
And osier brook and grassy rivulet mild.
Happy the babe that naught of mortal ill
Save parting pang inherits ; rathe beguiled
To cast aside life's burden garb of clay,
And, careless, tireless, sinless, wait the doom.
Yet breaks the mother's heart, strive as she may
To gild with pious after-hope her gloom.

Thus Hester mourned like Rachel, all her prayer
For welcome death to ease her of the load
That grew too hard for gentle soul to bear.
Moved by her sorrow, Moore contrition showed
Awhile, but, doglike, soon returned again
To his foul vomit, drink.
                              A month went by,
And tidings came of further loss.   In vain
He sought to borrow.   All were cold and shy.
How matters not, he yet had come to know
Of Gray's bequest, the ring and privy store ;
And now would oft entreat his wife to go
And somewhat claim of need.   But she, the more
He urged, refused , for all her soul rebelled
To take to traitor use benignant gold.
So grew constraint to open breach.   Repelled
Again ere long with resolute scorn, made bold
Of rage, he lift his coward hand and smote
The wife he vowed to cherish.
                                      Night was come,
And all about was peaceful.   Jocund note
Came from adjacent cot, uncareful home
Where wedded maid, proud mother but of late,

Her cradled joy sang lightsome to its rest.
Well Hester knew the singer, frequent mate
In happy, guileless girlhood.   Swelled her breast
With sense of wrong to madness.   Death alone
Could loose the marriage tie so vilely gained,
And end life's ills, both present and unknown.
One look she gave her tyrant, then, constrained
Of agony, fled forth the house and sought
The singer's shelter.   Here her fevered head
She laid on friendly breast, until she caught
Her husband's voice anew, and, shuddering, fled,
Pursued by oath and threat.   In deep despair
She fled unheedful whither, till the dash
Of water 'gainst the uneven causey stair,
Smote on her ear with dull and mournful plash.

The night was clear, the river murmurous ran
Back to the breast of all embraceful sea ;
Like babe that, mother-parted little span,
Babbling delight, with eager-footed glee
Speeds to her arms to lose in love's embrace
Record of loss in whirl of frantic joy.
Gaunt in the night, its stern and felly face
The regal keep uplift, yet still—alloy
Of soul-oppressive gloom—shone here and there
A turret light, like beacon star in murk.
She now upon the brink, in wild despair,
Wringing her hands, intent life's cruel irk
To end, self-slain, a last sad look around
Cast, ere she sought the solace of the flood.

Now dull across the stream the clangous sound
Of ship-bell swept ; while hard by where she stood
Rose sailor shout in rude responsive hail.
Disturbed, she drew aside, as plash of oar
Spake nearing boat ; and, hidden, 'What avail
Is death to me, he living still, who more
Should die for evil done than guiltless I
For ill sustent !'
               So flashed the pregnant thought
Through maddened brain : ' The rather let me fly.
I have the ring.   Ah, love ! long time I've fought
'Gainst love and thee, of duty. What reward
Hath right, all things subservient to wrong ?'
Now ground the boat against the shelvy hard.
The men got in with snatch of ribald song,
Timing the throb of oar. Alone, again
She stood upon the stair, the plaining stream
Dark at her feet slow lapsing to the main.
Head bent, hands clasped, long hung she, deathful dream
Still in her brain. At length : ' Dear love, I'll take
Enough to-morrow of thy gold—enough,
No more, and that unwilling, for thy sake,
To hie me far away. Though rude and rough
My life henceforth, I shall at least be free
From drunken mate, revilings, cursings, blows.'
Here fell the teardrops of her misery
Fast in the stream. ' The veriest wretch that goes
Hungry from vil to vil hath happier fate.
What harm, then, have I done, what ill, what sin ?'
Repentant now she homeward turned. The gate
Was open, and the cottage dark within.

He, then, was absent, so she grateful crept
In solitude and darkness to her bed.
Here lay she wakeful of distress, nor slept
For long time, then, disturbed by noisy tread,
Waked startling. Once more 'twas her tyrant sot
Returning drunken ! Cursing, grumbling, came,
Oft stumbling on the stair, the vinous blot
On manhood, honest husband's sorriest shame.

Cold as the beam that pierced the dormer pane,
And checkered ceil and floor and wainscot bare,
She trembling lay, like fawn on grassy plain,
Lost from the leafy covert's homely lair.
He coming, brutal, struck her cruel blow,
And yet again with oathings foul, and word
Of shame more hard to bear than utmost throe
Of pain—by virtuous wife—or stake, or sword ;
Then fell where late he fell and did to death
His babe, and, falling, struck his head, and lay
Prone at her feet.

    *   *   *   *   *

               The morrow's fragrant breath
Breathed through the casement. Soon the flame of day
Filling the chamber, girt the sleeping man,
Who stirred not, nor when all the down awoke
Made waking sign. Alarmed, now Hester ran
To seek a neighbour. Soon the calm was broke
By exclamation, eager, shrill, and oft.
Dead where he fell he lay, his cruel face
Kissing the stone, the marble stone more soft
Than his own cruel heart.

Imbuted trace
Yet on her brow and breast of drunkard hand,
Few said 'Heaven rest him !' while the most perceived
God's wrathful judgment, shown in swift command
To Death, His creature's course of ill achieved.

V.

Ere long returned anew her faithful swain,
The richer for his venture ; and still more
Intent on love, his sweetheart's woes and· pain
Learned from the common converse. She was poor
That once was rich ; and wan, whose maiden cheek
Had shamed the rose; while suffering out her eyes
Had stol'n the god-light. Thoughtful, silent, meek,
She moved as one o'ercome of miseries.
His brave heart bled to see it ; thousand-fold
His love increased of pity, yet in vain
From day to day he pleaded. Love untold
Spake in her eyes, yet could he nothing gain
But this : 'It is not meet that I should mate
With whom I once was faithless.'

So she said,
Long time to each entreaty. They that wait,
Nor falter in pursuit, to conquest head
Do bring endeavour. Thus true love at last
Obtained well-won reward. Once more the bells
Whirled mad-tongued in their lair. Of trouble past
And livelong bliss begun, the pæan swells
With sore tried hearts long parted, beat for beat
Rapturous pulsing; while Nepenthe draught

The young loves mix at Hymen-banquet sweet,
And Cupid, gleeful, wings ecstatic shaft.

Now came again the bloom to Hester's cheek.
Again her beauty knew its earlier charm,
While Fortune, as repenting cruel freak,
Sought every way resentment to disarm.
So lived they happy, naught alone withheld,
But gift of babbler offspring.   Yet would fall
Betimes on Hester horror gloom, dispelled
By spousal tenderness, redoubled all
By piteous remembrance of the past.
Of nights, too, sometimes waked of nameless fears,
Her cry would thrill her sleeping mate, who, fast
Clasping her trembling form, would chide the tears
And sobs of deep-set sorrow.
                              Years went by—
Full fraughted years—that saw a royal head
Fall at a nation's anger.   Tyranny
In one overthrown, in many wider spread
To quicker judgment.   Then the common debt
Gray paid, bequeathing all his ample store
To Hester.   She ere long from vain regret
Found solace in good deeds.   Thus many a sore
And aching heart she comforted, the thought
Of once o'erpowering sorrow winging aid,
The ampler, readier, and full oft unsought,
To widow, babe, or all too yielding maid
That should be wife, but was not.
                              Most of all,
She loved to meet the boys at eventide—

The winsome, gamesome boys released from thrall
Of task and schoolhouse.   They their noisy pride
Bated at her approach, not seldom bow
Or book or ball the prize to him that best
Made answer to her quest'ning.   Who could know,
Save one as desolate, how full her breast
Of motherhood and sympathy for aught
That still was young and harmless ?   Warning word
She sometime spake, lest heedlessness were fraught
With cruelty, or treach'ry should be sword
To pierce confiding heart.
                         By all revered,
Thus lived she till, upon her comely head
Time laying rimy hand, the snow appeared—
White ensign of the kingdom of the dead
That the dark portal silent opening shows.
Already they that shared her youthful past,
And knew her after-lot of mis'ry, blows,
Save one or two, had entered in the vast
Unstoried region.   She the approaching day
Waited, but not unfearful, frequent prayer
And kindly deed redoubling, vestured clay
Shrinking perforce from Death's relentless share.

VI.

The summer sun, sky-wearied, drew to close,
Its red rays slanting seaward o'er the stream,
What time some life-worn trav'ler sought repose
From heirloom toil and hope's fallacious dream
Within the peaceful have of Terra's breast.

Dull, deep, and slow the bell boomed out the tale,
By sexton urged, the while a mate addrest
His sinewy strength to delve the clayey pale.
His task well-nigh complete, a fleshless skull
He careless threw without his deepening den ;
This, rolling down the rugged slope, made dull
And curious rattling. One slow pacing then
The churchyard path, the pastor newly called
To parish cure, saw where the death's head fell,
And, drawing nearer, raised it ; but, appalled,
A moment after dropped the mouldering cell
With cry of horror. Shuddering once again
He took the gruesome emblem.
                                        ' Murder vile,'
He muttered awestruck, ' here is writ full plain,
And plain revealed ! And yet what end ? Long while
Ago the deed was done. This rusted nail,
Fast harboured where it clave its deadly way,
A lifetime since was driven. Who the tale
Dare hope to fathom ? Lives the wretch to-day ?
Or has the doom he dealt been judged by Him
Who, judging all men righteously, doth fill
His cup of vengeance ever to the brim
For them that, impious, dare His image spill ?
But yet the man is old. Perchance the name
Of him this tell-tale wreck doth represent
May linger.'
                    So, the skull in hand, he came
Nearer the chasm, and attentive bent
Over the delver, making question. He
For answer pored upon a battered plate

Red-rusted : 'Ay, the name's here, if so be
I could but read it ! Ne'er my shallow pate
Could hold much learning. First an O, and next
Another. Then there comes——' The sexton here
Stood gaping, scratching head, as sore perplext.
Meanwhile the priest, with brow and look severe,
Impatient waited : 'Prithee, Diggory, pass
The plate to me,' he said at length, and laid
The death's head down among the nettled grass.
'Why now for sure,' the old man chuckling said,
' 'Tis Moore—'tis Moore that married Hester Gray.
To think I had forgotten ! Well, 'tis nigh
On forty years, if 'tis a blessed day ;
Will Moore that died in drunken fit.' A cry
Brake from the frowning priest. 'A drunken fit !'
He scornful muttered ; 'ay, but deadly nail
To hinder waking !'
                                 He within the pit,
Uplooking, saw the priest was wondrous pale,
And honest questioned. 'Nay, a qualm—no more,'
The priest returned ; 'a passing qualm ! But, see,
Your aguish task is done, or most ; give o'er.
This relic takes my fancy. Come with me ;
A stoup of ale will stave off marish ill ;
Dame Woodward shall provide it !'
                                            Nothing loath,
The man clomb forth : 'Now tell me, an you will,'
The priest continued, while an idle cloth
He wrapped about the skull, 'whate'er you know
Of Moore, his end, and Mistress Hester Gray.'
So did the man, oft pausing, doubtful, slow,
The tale full long escaped from memory's sway.

VII.

The morrow came. 'Twas stormy; drifting rain—
That soddened all the down, and drave the kine
To hovel shelter—'gainst the streaming pane
Beat furious; while the jasmine's shivering vine
Wept in the wind, that smote the elm-tops tall
This way and that tyrannic. Howling swept
The gale about the eaves. The gabled wall
Shook in the drift. The mastiff, growling, crept
The deeper in his kennel, restless aye,
And rattling chain uneasy. Overhead
The vane incessant twirled with long-drawn sigh,
Or goblin shriek rebellious. Sore bestead,
All day the bully sparrow chirped reproof
Of wind and rain within his ivy nest;
While, home-kept in his mansion, 'neath the roof
The white-winged swallow preened his spotless breast.

At noon, the storm abating, Hester sat,
As was her wont, within the cushioned seat
That filled the deepset casement. Grassy plat,
And lilac grove, and trellised arbour neat
Were as of yore; for Gray the gardened cot,
His wife's first home, had bought again; no place
So dear by half as that, the blissful spot
Where, equal love confest, her blushing face
Was laid upon his shoulder. Oft indeed
Would rise in each remembrance of the strife
'Twixt love and right, when bitter fate decreed
Lover and mistress, sore-deceived wife,

Perforce must part, or drag unholy chain
Of passion bondage, heavier day by day.
Small pain the remembrance brought, rich after gain
Of joy allaying thought of sorrow's sway.

Within the window Hester sat, for long
Absorbed in page of old black-lettered tome,
Open upon her lap at plaintive song
Of Israel's royal penitent, that home,
Age after age, speaks to each heart that yoke
Unwilling bears of ill—corrective doom!
Now lifting up her pensive eyes, she spoke,
Tearful, the prophet words.
              Yet deeper gloom
Fell on the world without, and forth a cloud
Leapt lightning, but afar, with muttering mate
Slow toiling after.   Prayerful, Hester bowed
Her head upon her book.   But now, the gate
Loud clanging, strode the minister in haste
Up the dank path.   Unwelcome visitant
The man to most.   In early days unchaste,
Ribald, and lax; complaisant ministrant
Of ill to all; reformed, none more severe
To young and old alike, did any swerve
But hair's breadth from his standard.   Yet sincere
The man was, doubtless, thinking to subserve
God's ends by sternness.
              Hester saw him now
Not pleased, his harshness on her kindlier mood
Jarring continual.   Still, intent to show
Due honour to his office, ris'n she stood

Expectant by the window, while her maid
Unlatched the outer door.   Stern-visaged he
And cold, as one that half reluctant played,
Of duty, painful part ; her courtesy
He met with small acknowledgment, and took
A seat somewhat apart.   Silent a space,
He slow began, his eyes with searching look
Ever upon her, watchful, seeking trace
Of fear, confusion, or impallid dread
At guilt brought home a-sudden.

       ' Mistress Gray,
Last eve the sexton, delving grave, o'erspread
The churchyard path with upturned mould and clay.
A skull, thrown careless up, rolled close to feet.
I, moved of curious whim, took up the wreck,
And, making question, heard the man repeat
A story of much import.   Little reck
Wrongdoers of the God that vengeth ill,
But impious frame a proverb, "Dead men tell
No tales," and thus do bolden murderous will
To deed, and think with pause of funeral bell
Discovery at end.'

      So said he slow,
And watchful of the effect his studied words
Should have on Hester.   But her snow-crowned brow,
Untroubled, showed no sign of terror chords
Thrilling within her.   Frowning, spake again
Her stern-souled visitant : ' These forty years
And more the deed was done ; but still 'tis plain
The man was murdered.   Yea, his skull appears,
Witness immatchable to prove the crime,

And bring to righteous judgment her that slew
With monster hand her husband.'
                                    Other time
Again he paused ; but ever greater grew
Perplexity and doubt within his soul,
For Hester sat, untouched, untroubled still,
As hearing pointless tale.   Alone there stole
Strange smile to eye and lip, as but the will
Were wanting to bemock stultiloquence.
Then fiercely he again : ' Your husband Moore,
I say, was murdered.   Speak your innocence !
Woman, unlock those callous lips before
I hale thee forth to prison and to duom !
Dost know this rusted nail ?   From out the skull
Of William Moore I wrenched it.'
                                    Hurtling boom
Of o'erhead thunder here, with uproar dull,
Drowned further accusation.
                              Painful, slow,
White as the lambskin laid on window floor,
Hester uprose, and spake the one word, ' Go !'
Pointing with trembling hand the parlour door.
Now, furious, he : ' Woman, I go ; beware
My rathe return !'
                    Again the storm brake forth ;
But he, fierce anger conquering self, no care
Took of the failing tempest's fitful wrath,
But, stern, self-chosen blood-avenger, made,
Through rain and blast and hurtling thunder-peal,
To claim the scoffing tipstaff's grudgeful aid.
Hester the while with overwhelming reel

Of mind and brain, low crouched, her whirling brow
Laid on the seat.
                      'Ah, God ! Thou knowest all !—
It cannot be ! Thou knowest ! Naught I know
But that I woke at sound of hammer fall.
Most merciful ! I thanked Thee then no ill
My witless hand had worked him. Can it be
E'en then that hand ? Hence, awful thought ! Be still,
My heart, or kill in leaping. Pity me,
Dear Lord ! A nail within his brain—a nail !
'Twas Jael drove it ! Jael, I ! No, no !
Not murderess vile ! Oh, horror !'
                                      Wail on wail
Surged from her soul in bitterness of woe,
Till brake her harmless heart of misery.
Once more a cry, ' O Jesu, grant relief !'
And Hester Gray lay dead of agony,
Christ of His pity stilling heart and grief.
          *   *   *   *   *
The storm passed by. The sun's impatient ray,
Parting the hindering clouds, sped hasty down
On angel errand, till, where Hester lay,
Lovingly entering in, effulgent crown
It laid upon her restful.

BALLAD.

My sweeting is queen of the ball!
    Sing hey for the light in her eyes,
The blush on her cheek and her innocent brow,
Her cherry lip chaste and her bosom of snow,
    Her feet, oh so shapely and small!

My sweeting is queen of the ball!
    Sing hey for the lift of her breast,
Her smile that is brighter than sunbeam at morn,
Her sigh that is softer than zephyr forlorn,
    Love-lonely in Æolus' hall!

My sweeting is queen of the ball!
    Sing hey for the gleam of her feet,
That now from their covert of camelot peep,
Now hide them, coquettish, now gracefully sweep
    The floor at Terpsichore's call!

My sweeting is queen of the ball!
    Ah me, that no part have I there!
Another my lady may tenderly clasp,
Another her dainty hand loverly grasp,
    Be suitor, and partner, and thrall!

Yet, sweeting, be queen of the ball!
    Dance on, my own darling, be gay;
For life is but labour, and sorrow will beat
Too soon at youth's portal—will leaden the feet
    That now so bewitchingly fall!

RAHERE.

I.

THE thunder rolled ! The rain in sleety waves
Dashed at the pane, impelled of fury blasts
That shrieking raged about the ruined pile,
As eager to complete man's mindless wreck.
The lightning clave the concave of the sky,
With far-resounding shock that wrapped the world
A moment in wild uproar, deafening, vast—
Father of after-silence—till the ear,
Regaining office, heard the exultant storm
Rage fiercer, as the glorious face of earth
It hated, and insensate would deform
In very pride of hate.
                        The glooms of eve
Had gathered, but the larger darkness born
Of overhanging tempest filled the fane
With deeper shade. The low-arched aisles were full
Of darkness, veiling tablet, wall, and tomb.
Yet still within the apse the pillars vast
Stood out like broad-browed giants, spreading wide
Their arching arms, uplifting realms of stone
So massy as to mock at Time and storm—
So strong that only hand of man might mar
What hand of man upreared. Deep set above

Within the quarry wall, the clearstore lights—
Like mouths of flame, or furnace doors wide thrown,
Revealing fervent worlds—shone out whene'er
The livid bolt outleapt the tempest womb
With throe of thunder.
                              Ceaseless dashed the rain
'Gainst roof and wall and casement.   Lurid flashed
The storm-born messenger of flame.   The roll
Of wrathful thunder yet and yet again
Woke all the hundred echoes of the fane.
Unceasing wailed the wind through arch and aisle,
Unearthly 'mid the darkness.   Yet there knelt
Beside the founder's tomb, within the choir,
A maid, and prayed regardless of the storm—
Black-robed, white-coifed, with long and lustrous hair,
That, fallen, lay about the holy ground.
So still she knelt upon the pavement stone,
Time-worn and stained, some chiselled effigy
She seemed of saint absorbed in blessed prayer.

Anon a fiercer flame uplighting all
With blinding ray, she slowly lift her head,
And, rising, laid her head upon the tomb.
' From lightning and from tempest, Lord, we pray,
Deliver us !   Yet ever nearer Thee
I seem whene'er Thy lightning giveth shine,
And feel Thou dost but speak me in the storm.
What terror now has tempest strife for him
That sleeps beneath this fretted canopy ?
In Thee quiescent, all his travail done,

Shakes earth, falls heav'n, he peaceful sleeps, nor heeds.
So I, firm stayed on Thee, what dread for me
Lurks in Thy bolt, or hides in hurricane?
So dost Thou but abandon crystal throne
To visit earth on wings of mighty winds ;
Thine awful presence told in meteor flight,
Or quake of elements that own Thee Lord.
Yet shame to us, sweet Lord, we too should fear
Thy creature children fashioned in Thy face !'

So said the maid and smiled, her steadfast gaze
Set on the lofty casement's changeful pane.
But now amid the peace that followed shock,
A timid voice, appealing, called, ' Rahere !
Rahere ! Rahere ! Dear sister, where art thou ?'

A door there was within the sombre aisle,
Of sculptured stone, the work of sometime prior,
Whose rebus artful filled the tympanum
Amid congenial foliage of the vine.
The door wide-thrown, a beam of flickering light
Streamed out a chamber, and within the ray
A child stood calling. Naked were the feet,
Chilled of the furrowed sill, and pale, that peeped
Without her gown of dimity, and bare
The pretty rounded arm, outstretched, that spoke
Itself entreaty ; while her loosened hair,
Black as the night, lay shimmering on her breast,
That rose and fell distressful.
                              At the sight,
Seen through the massy apsis columns, quick

Her thoughts recalled to lowlier things, the maid
Forsook the shrine to clasp the child in arms.
'Why shouldst thou fear, Cecilia? Yet is mine
The fault, and thine, dear child, the right to chide.
But thou wert sleeping, and the tempest broke
While yet I knelt beside the prior's tomb :
So beautiful the lightning's fervid play,
The booming thunder's deep sepulchral call,
I could not draw away from spirit strife
That spoke my soul with hundred kindred tongues.
But thou art cold! My pretty one, thy breath
Comes doubtful, while thou tremblest like to leaf
New born, and touched with soft mysterious joy
At being and to be in such fair world.
Come back to bed. I'll sit beside thee till
The storm gives o'er, or life's best comrade, sleep,
Seals up anew those fear-distended eyes.'
So said Rahere, and bore the trembling child
Close nuzzling to her breast again to rest.

Not all destroyed the prior's stately home.
Though much decayed and broken, yet there stood
A fragment still against the chancel wall,
With vaulted chambers low, and windows deep
Embrasured in the rubble parquetry—
So deep the sun might hardly enter in
The pillared cell and mote th' uneven floor.
The sisters here were born ; but first Rahere,
Alarmed at day, had joyed her mother's ear
With babeling cry delightful. Grown to girl,

And Death that mother claiming ere Cecile
Could prattle forth endearing tenderness,
Rahere was mother, sister, both in one,
And none e'er truer.   Sped the years, and now
Rahere to woman grown, death smote again
With urgent stroke the portal of their home,
And bade away its husband.   So the maid
Was left to urge life's warfare hazardous
Unfriended, but with dower of beauty, oft
More ban than benediction, bane than good.

Cecilia laid again within her bed,
Her arms fast set about her sister's neck,
Spake softly now, her dread a little past :
' I could not sleep, Rahere, the cruel storm
So fearful raging.   See that dreadful flash !
Forgive me ; have I called you needlessly—
But—but Rahere—again that horrid crash !
You say 'tis God a-speaking in the storm.
Why should He speak so loud ?   Your voice is soft,
Rahere, so soft ; I never weary, dear,
Whene'er you speak, whate'er it be you say.'
With loving hand the clammy upturned brow
Rahere smoothed gently, then made calm reply :
' God speaks, Cecile, in ways and tones untold ;
Some hear Him when the aspens, murmurous, make
Their melody at bid of wakening breeze ;
Some when the bright-winged sunbeams kiss the face
Of smiling earth.   Again, some others best
When Night with lifted finger hushes Day,

And brooding stillness coverlets the world ;
Some when the mild waves lap the shelvy shore,
And murmur, "Sister-sands, we come again ;
Have ye no welcome ?"   Some, alas ! Cecile,
Will never heed Him till He ding as now,
And shake their souls through coward ears that throb
In anxious consternation.   All His tones
To them that love Him, sweet, are beautiful,
And all His ways delightful.'
                              Here Cecile,
Faint smiling, answered : ' Then, indeed, I fear
I love Him not, or not as you.   I find
No beauty in the tempest.   Sing me now,
Rahere ; your voice, at least, I understand :
Sing, sister, till the tiresome storm is o'er.'

    Sleep, sister ! what and if the tempest beat
        Fierce at thy chamber pane ;
    Though lightnings flash through whirl of rain and
        sleet,
        And thunders shake the fane !
    Sleep on, thy sister sits beside thy bed ;
    Sleep on, good angels guard thy guiltless head !

    Sleep, sister ! so the gentle Lord of all,
        Worn with the day's distress,
    A-slumbered lay the while the tempest-call
        Shook with its fearfulness
    Sea, ship, and them whose souls the hissing wave
    Thrilled with the threat of wild and wat'ry grave !

Sleep, sister ! fiercer still the tempests rave,
  Yet does He calmly sleep.
' Wake, Master, wake ! Save, Lord, we perish—save !
  Death dwells within the deep !'
He wakes, He smiles, He lifts His sacred hand—
' Peace, peace !' and all is still at His command.

Sleep, sister ! still the same dear Lord doth wait
  But for His people's prayer,
And if betimes He seem to sleep, their fate
  Yet is His tireless care.
For them the storm, for them He quells the sea,
Rules flood and flame, supreme in sovranty.

The sweet voice sank to silence ; then Cecile
The singer's face drew down, till loving lips
Met in the music of impassioned kiss.
So lay they for awhile, then spoke Rahere,
Her words first prefaced by a heavy sigh
And lingering caressing : ' Darling, now
I have a matter I had thought to keep
Till morning from thee. Yonder posy still
Is fresh and wholesome. How o'erjoyed we were
To pluck it yester eve in Pancras fields
With alehoof and the first sweet sprig of may !
Thy lappet apron full, dost call to mind
The wish our home were ever in the fields
Anigh a wood ? Nay, heed no more the storm,
'Tis passing ; that was but a farewell shock.
Cecile, my sweet, there is a home for thee
In field and wood—a little way removed,

8

In truth, but not so far I may betimes
Come see thee and remain with thee awhile.'

More had she said, but here the child, alarmed,
Sprang up, and, careless all of wind and storm,
Knelt in her cot and looked Rahere in face.
'Betimes come see me! nay, I'll nowhere go,
Rahere, where you are not.   'Twould be no home
Without you, sister.   I'd ne'er see a field
Or flower again so I might stay with you!
You cannot mean it, sister.'
                                        To her heart
Rahere drew close the sobbing supplicant,
And spake her gently, while her sorrow rained
A tear-shower on her tresses.   'Home, alas!'
She sighed, 'we have no more to call our own;
This crumbling roof, endeared—ah me, how dear!—
By years of childish happiness, nor less
By mem'ries of the dead, and goodly thoughts
Born of the prayerful cloister's solemn calm,
Is ours alone of charity awhile,
And ours no more whene'er the presbyter,
Who takes our father's place, assumes the cure.
Then must we forth, and I must work, Cecile,
If I would eat, as saith the holy Paul,
And gladly also had done so for thee
Had need been; but from Tott'ridge comes reply
From Master Hale our uncle.   Home there is
For thee with him.   But I—well, I am grown
To woman, and must work.   Dear heart, 'tis right,
And doubtless for the best, that thou shouldst go,

Though bitter hard our parting. Yet the night—
The last night of his life—our father bade
Me write our aunt, his sister, on his part,
And this comes back.'
                              At this Cecilia wept
Anew within her sister's jealous arms ;
'But must I go, Rahere? Nay, sister, nay !
Still keep me with you ; I'll not fear for storm,
Nor vex you ever, only let me stay.'

'It may not be, alas !' Rahere replied,
With effort brave at firmness, only now
And then her breath came gasping, while a sob
Brake from her spite endeavour. 'Nay, Cecile,
In sooth to part is bitterness supreme ;
But yet, dear child, I give thee up to God,
And pleasant future, safe, and well assured ;
'Twas out of grief, indeed, I sought the church
And tomb of him of whom I bear the name.
And praying there for comfort, came the storm,
And strangely, with its breaking, sorrow passed
Away as God Himself uplift my soul.
Cecile, my thoughts have ever been to thee
Since first our mother died, but doubly since
Death bade our father home to larger sphere
Of service in his Master's land of light ;
So now I may not balance tenderness
In scale with duty. 'Tis His blessed will,
And I submit. But, darling, ne'er forget
I do it but of honest love for thee.
Now lay thee down and sleep, if so thou canst.

Be sure Rahere will never fail in love,
But, shouldst thou prove unhappy in thy home,
Thy newer home, will surely fetch thee thence
Whate'er her lot.'
                    With lingering kiss and sigh
The child lay down.   Rahere with streaming eyes
Bent o'er her mournful, while the storm swept by
With lessening gale and distant thunder-peal.

II.

Within the prior's pew, high set, between
The bold triforium's pillared archings rude,
Two men stood watchful, thoughtful.   One in dress
Sad coloured, as became God's servitor,
Gazed down with knitted brow and look austere
Upon Rahere, who nigh the founder's tomb
Sat sewing, all unconscious of the eyes
That jealous marked her every stir and mien.
By far the elder this.   The other, young
And richly drest though simply, smiling gazed
Large-eyed as one astonished, ne'er displeased.
Some while they gazed.   Then softly urged the youth,
' Who is the maid, good Master Hope?   Too dull
Her garb for angel.   Were she but in white,
As poets pen and painters limn the saints,
Nor plying needle over mortal wear,
Methinks she might beseem some happy ghost
Or saintly patroness of this old fane.'

' Tush, Master Hewett!   Tush!   what speech is this?
Some saintly patroness!   Malignant lips

Might frame the words, but never godly youth.'
So said the presbyter, and deeper frowned
The while upon the maid, whose lovely head,
Uplifted now, was laid against the shrine.
'I crave your pardon, Master Hope,' the youth
Made answer gently, though contemptuous look
First curled his mobile lips.   'But, see, the maid
Is weeping.   Surely, now 'twere godly part
To play the minister l'
                                          'The maid has cause
To weep,' replied the presbyter, 'her heart,
I fear, not firmly set upon the Lord.
Her father, one time slave to prelacy,   ,
My predecessor in the cure, did sign
The Covenant, but not of conscience' sake,
But, as is common talk, for love of her
Who sits by yonder shard of Popery,
And other younger daughter.   He of late
Gone to the judgment waiting Demas souls,
Rahere perforce must win her daily bread.'

'Rahere,' the youth repeated, thoughtfulwise ;
'Is't not the name of him that built the church,
King Beauclerk's minstrel ?'   'Yea, the very same,
And so canst somewhat gauge the mind of him
Who could so name his daughter, after lewd
And godless maker of unholy songs.'
'In sooth 'twas strange, yet have I ever heard
Of penitence Rahere did build the church
And hospice l   So may be——'   Thus far the youth,
When, stern and hot, the presbyter rejoined :

'Ay, ay! too oft doth Satan glozen souls
To deeper doom by mammon hope to win
Forgiven entrance to celestial home,
E'en at the last, by fallacy of works,
Most deadly of all errors!'
                           Coldly here
The youth made answer: 'Surely, Master Hope—
Your pardon an I speak you overbold—
'Tis better to repent, with honest proof
Of reformation in some goodly deed,
Than idle prate of faith and charity
With never sign of either, first or last.'

Sore vexed at speech so plain, with barb of truth
Adjoined, the presbyter made sharp reply:
'Such speech doth ill become your father's son,
And my good friend.   It cannot be you hold
With prelacy or Independent crew.
Sir Edward must be warned.'   But here the youth
As sternly interposed: 'In truth, good sir,
I had my father in my thought, and so
Spake that I spake!   Is't not the common saw
At Beech Hill, and of him, "The longer prayer,
The lesser ruth"?   Doth not he preface mean
And covetous oppression of the folk
That service him alone through hap of birth,
With Scripture garnish text and monologue?
You, too, are much his debtor.   Have you found
Your schoolmate friend less urgent of his due
Than veriest Hebrew?   E'er put off a day
Demand of payment?   Wherefore am I here?

What is't I bear him back but usury,
And usury enforcèd of a friend?
My father! Well, enough of him. You know
Him, as I know; I had not spoken else.
You were, methinks, about to tell me more
Of yonder weeping maid?'
                                    'Nay, nothing more
Save that she gains a meagre livelihood,
E'en as you see, and comes o' times to work
Of phantasy beside her namesake's tomb.
She hath strange likings, and of late doth lie
Within the gate beyond the outer field,
For love of godless shadows, monk and knight;
Her sister gone to care of worthy friends;
Her mother dead, and kindred wide dispersed.'

A mournful look o'erspread the young man's face:
'No sister—mother! 'Tis a hapless lot;
Mine too, and, truth, no blow can hammer heart
To agony like that of loss of her
Who makes home, home. Our fathers were but fools
To call man husband. Often 'tis the wife's
Sweet unassertive presence that doth bind
All lives in one, and watchful draw around
Unquiet souls the cords of peace and love.
Without her house may be, but never home;
My mother, life is not since thou didst die!'
So sighed the youth. The minister was moved
To gentle answer: 'Lad, thou speakest truth—
In part, at least! So, so—we'll jar no more.'

Rahere, meanwhile, her grief o'erpast again,
Took up her broider task.   But now the sun,
Sometime obscured by passing cloud, brake forth,
And falling full on wall and floor, the rays
Gilt with their golden beauty all the fane;
And looking up, with sad but raptured eyes,
She sighing stretched her hands towards the beam :
' My God ! my God ! how beautiful Thou art !
Thy lesser world so fair, how glorious
Thy star-girt home !   Ah me l were I with Thee !'
Beholding this, the presbyter again
Frowned deeply, slowly shaking reverend head,
Her words not heard.   Far otherwise the youth.
He at the sight was moved, he knew not why,
To sympathy of sorrow.   Turning now,
He urged the other mildly : ' Master Hope,
Shall we not speak the maid ?   But charity
To help her in her strait, if so may be ;
Come, go we down !'
                    Thus urged, the presbyter
Unwilling turned, yet fain had made excuse,
Had reason served.   Scarce down the oaken stair,
Came one in haste, to bid the minister
To conference with newly-come divines.
' Nay, never make excuse,' the youth rejoined,
To proffered courtesy.   ' I'll wait you here.
This ponderous door should open on the church ;
I'll walk within awhile.'
                    The old man's face
Was lit with meaning smile, as slow he went
To join his strait-laced brethren, parlour set :

' The maid is comely. Fever-blooded youth,
Vainwarned, will ever seek the sirens' isle,
And, heedless there of whitening bone and wreck,
Will madly near to list the deadly song !'

Alone the youth uplift the brazen catch
With careful hand, and softly oped the door :
' Now may I find the maid, and find her still
Thought-spelled and rapt, as now when I beheld
Her lovely face than Niobe's more sad !
Nay, she has moved, yet every movement grace,
Sweet girl, and should thy lesser self enshrine
But half so fair a soul, my heart, I fear,
Henceforth is in thy keeping.'
                                     Coming now
With lissom tread across the chancel aisle,
He made Rahere obeisance : ' Maiden, now
Your pardon for intrusion.   Much, I fear,
Iconoclast unwilling of fair thoughts,
I come unwelcome.'   So he said, his words
Well chos'n and tagged with due sincerity,
Which she perceiving, ' Sir, the church is free,'
Returned him gently, making reverence,
' To all alike that love its restful aisle
And solemn calm, remote from all that jars
Our goodlier being.'
                          ' Lady, I am one,'
The youth replied, ' who loves the peace you praise,
And praise most justly.   Yet are men but men,
At strident voice of duty bound to range
Themselves this side or that.   Were all men priests

Or scholars, wedded only to their books,
The world would fare but badly; beauty waste,
And fail God-given purpose.' Here he bowed;
She, blushing, changed the theme to other speech
With woman wit. 'You came to see the church;
Was it not so? I'll gladly be your guide;
My father late was vicar.'
                                    Overjoyed
To have such guide, the youth made fit reply;
But cautious, gauging well her virgin soul,
Mistrustful. Now from aisle to aisle they went;
She, artless, all her lore of stone and tomb
Revealing, glad of sympathetic mind;
He dwelling rapt on untaught eloquence,
And feeding, silent, on th' unstudied charm
Of trembling lip and kindling cheek and eye.

Now came they once again beside the tomb
Where slept Rahere, and here the maiden stood
A short while thoughtful. Then, in doubtful wise,
First glancing at her comrade, slowly spake,
A tremor in her voice, as one that speaks
Moved of a righteous anger in defence
Of absent friend or lover:
                                    ' This one tomb
I kept of purpose till the last, as first
Of all—indeed, our chiefest ornament.
Here rests Rahere, disparaged much of some
Who deeper see not than the glistering fringe
Of giddy foam that flecks the ocean's breast,
Conceiving not the vast and mighty waste

Of water peaceful as the grave that girds
Earth everywhere about in fold eterne,
Deep-set, unseen, emotionless as Death.
Men are but men, set all about with snares
And lures, and pitfalls dug of ghostly shapes,
And powers recalcitrant. Assaulted thus,
All fall, some more, some less ; some few, like swine,
Persistent wallow in their wantonness ;
While good men break away sometime, and soar
The loftier for their soilure. Is't not true,
Great lives of great denials most do come ?
So 'twas at least with him whose effigy
Doth here so sweetly pardon supplicate.
For he was rich—in favour with his king—
Love plighted—famous in the lists of song,
And as I doubt not in the lists of men ;
For kings they love not cowards. Read you now,
'Tis here upon his tomb full plainly writ,
How much he took in barter, and for these
The things men cherish most, and, seeking, oft
Will wear away the well-spring of their lives—
"Primus canonicus." And Prior priest
God-vowed and dedicate, of this his gift
To Him, His Church and people.'
                                        Thus Rahere,
In speech melodious, and that the more
The gentle indignation of her soul
Lent to her accents music. He awhile
Kept silence still, as loath to break the spell
The maiden, guileless, wove him all about.
Then with a sigh : ' I am your debtor much,

Sweet lady, and am one with you in thought ;
'Tis pity, too, such goodly pile should lie
Thus racked and spoiled.   Methinks the founder's soul
Must be sore vexèd, should vexation come
Within the portals of the wider world
Of waiting spirits.'
                              Quickly glancing round,
As fearful of eavesdropper, spake Rahere :
' Your dress, sir, speaks you Puritan ; your speech,
True Churchman.   Or—but no ! the very thought
Is too unworthy.   Treachery no place
Has in a manly heart.   I think you brave,
Or read your looks awry.   You would not seek
To frame for me displeasure out my speech ;
Of late too oft my portion has been more
Of chilling frowns than warmth of kindly looks.'

' A hundred ills the rather !' quick the youth
Made answer, and with vehemence ; ' I did
But honest speak the thought this shrine awoke
Within me.   Trust me, lady, all in all ;
An hour agone misspoke disparagement
I heard of him whose dust this fretwork holds,
And freely-urged objection.   As you say,
I am true Churchman.   When my mother died,
She, whisp'ring, spake me : " Edward, ne'er forsake
The one Church of your fathers."   Lady, I
Have ever kept her counsel firm in mind,
And so have never part with them that deem
Themselves th' elect, all else idolater.'

Now spake Rahere, emboldened : 'Once your thought
Was mine, and oft it grieved me, till one eve,
Not long since, as I sat within the gloom,
There brake upon me other : " He has joined
The larger host of souls emancipate,
And so has fuller knowledge, with disdain
Perchance, of much he counted much, so long
His ken was clogged by veil of earthiness.
Then followed this——" ' But here she paused, a look
Upon her lovely face all ardent lit,
As it should say : 'Rahere, thou art too bold
By far to prattle thus with stranger youth.'
' Nay, tell me all your mind,' anon he urged
With courteous entreaty. 'Mine I told.'
' This then my thought : Our minds so moved apart,
And oft by that would seem the closer bond ;
It cannot be the Lord of endless thought
And infinite conception doth restrain
His creatures to set worship. So they give
Him but His due, nor after other gods
Run blindly, them He leaves to choose the way
And method of their service. He that built
This church and hospice worshipped in the way
Our mothers loved and all our fathers taught.
Grapes burgeon not of thorns. ' Twas goodly deed
Thou didst, Rahere. If ours be good to give
This holy house to havoc—forging nails
On yonder noisy anvil, ringing loud
In desecrated transept—much more thine.
A child may batter that men scarce may build
So little recks Rahere of pomp and praise,

So long as prayer goes agelong up to Him
Who moved His servant's soul to raise the fane.'

More had she said, but now the presbyter,
With scholar cough, came slowly where they stood ;
So made the youth low-toned acknowledgment
Of service kindly render&d. She her task
Took up again with courteous rejoin,
And, rev'rence made to Master Hope, withdrew
Behind a pier to labour and to muse.

III.

Worn by the wing of Time, that year by year,
Slow-pulsing, robbed of sharpness, edge, and groin,
Yet proudly still bestriding all the way,
And darkly frowning, darklier still when storm
Beat at its 'brasures, stood the fortress gate,
Last shard of vast and stately English home,
Of them that erewhile manned the bloody breach
Against the Moslem thousand times, and won
Brief space Jerusalem and holy mount
To Christian ward and keeping.
                     Gone the knights
For ever ! Gone the prance of warrior steed,
Proud of his mail&d master ! Gone the flaunt
Of pennon and of plume, with clarion call
Ringing adown the courtyard, waking tramp
Of cross-clad knight and white-robed servitor
Obedient at its summons ! Floated more
No standard, haughty cognizance, that oft
Awed monarchs, and compelled unwilling praise ;

Ne'er castellan again, at blast of horn
Wound clam'rous at the gate, might welcome guest
From Araby or Malta, bearing tale
Of doughty deed against the Saracen.

Gone all! hushed all! The nearer life flows on
Less pompous, not less real. Life is life,
Though chivalry be legend of the past,
Be old-world tale, and pageantry depart
Like mist before the fuller blaze of day;
The nation lives and moves in upward course,
Or, doomful, downward, as its God decrees.

Yet stood the gate, though set to other use,
Yet never nobler, since within its walls
It sheltered now Rahere. A chamber small,
Within its western turret, served the maid
For sleeping; but the larger o'er the gate,
Disused and stored with ancient lumber, this
She loved, and here full oft the livelong day—
Debarred the church by spleen of Master Hope—
Would sit and labour at her broider tank.

Beneath the window blazon stood a chest
Fast locked, her seat; hard by a suit of mail,
With plumeless helm and rusted sheathless sword,
Was set against the wall. Anon the mood
Would take the maid to fashion him that wore
The battered panoply; his charger steed
That snorting shook the corse-heaped field; the flight
Of them that fled the flashing of the sword,
She, fearful of her darling, oft would touch

With timid finger, to her gentle thought
Each spot of rust the life-blood of a foe.

Nor only thus by day, but when the moon
Slid through the welkin cloudlets slow of flight,
To lap the gate in silver, peer within
Its dusty chambers dark with blackening oak,
And gild the broken trophies of the past
With its serene effulgence ; then Rahere,
Heart-thrilled, would seek the comfort of the ray,
Pure as her maiden self, and fearless sit
Beneath the pane, safeguarded as she deemed,
And may be not amiss, by soul of him
Who in his flesh had dwelt within the mail,
Christ-pledged to succour Holy Sepulchre, .
Grave matron, or sweet maiden in distress.

To-night so shone the moon.   Its gelid beam
Kissed, as it loved, the thoughtful maiden's brow,
Upturned to greet its splendour.   All around
Lay shadowy shapes of night.   The dull wind stirred
The tattered flag that, mouldering from the wall,
Hung listless, aimless.   Up the turret stair
Came moan of gust lugubrious, as if
Distressful shade of servitor or frere,
Unrestful, sighed its sorrow.
                                        All was still
Save for the breeze, and now the hour, that rolled
Slow from the old Carthusian belfry tower.
Eleven strokes deep boomed.   Rahere rose up.
' Now must I sleep, or day's impatient toil
Will wake me drowsy, aptless for its task.

And yet how calm, how lovely is the night !
Sure, Thou that madest darkness and the light
Hast doubly blest night's starry intervene
With larger presence of Thy seraph host.
How from their wings doth balm-like peace distil,
Refreshing hearts that ache from solitude,
Or loss of joy deep memoried, or stress
Of life-load proven all too burdensome !'

Here sighed the maiden deeply : ' Dost thou think
Betimes of me, Cecilia, in thy green
And pleasant home ?   My pretty one will draw
All hearts into her keeping.   Love to love
Must flow like springs to swell the billowy flood
That girdles earth.   To-night and dost thou sleep
Forgetful of thy sister, let my soul,
Strong of its passion, break its chain of flesh,
And free, of love awake thee, fill thine own
With gentle thoughts of her of whom thou ne'er
Didst have but gentle thinking.   Waken, sweet !
The same soft beam that lights me sorrowful
Falls on thee too.   Fair ray, my soul convey
To her, for I to-night am full of sad
And restless longings born of vanished joy.
Oh, were thine arms again about my neck !
Might I but feel thy kiss upon my lips,
And hear thy harmless prattle !'
                              Here the maid
Gave o'er abrupt, a choking in her throat.
' God save thee, sister, sleeping or awake !
Nor love nor hate His purpose may impede.

9

Lord, I believe; help Thou my unbelief!
Yet am I very lonely, come Thou near :
For Thou hast made me, and my spirit craves
Companionship—the craving Thou hast deep
Implanted in our souls for wisest end.'
So sighed she after, mistress of herself,
Within her chamber while she prayerful knelt.

But now a voice brake sudden into song
Beneath her window, whence her taper's light
Lost in the ampler fulgence of the moon,
Shone out but feebly.   All amazed at strain,
Unusual now that passing cavalier
Was mark by day for rabble discontent,
And roister wand'rer haled incontinent
O' nights by watch to lock-up or to cage,
Rahere arose, and, wondering, list the song.

SERENADE.

Raining down her silver gleam,
　　Out the welkin's cloudless height
Proud amid the lucent stream,
　　Rides the ray-crowned Queen of Night;
Fair is she, yet comes not near
My fair mistress, sweet Rahere !

Light from out her lattice flows,
　　Brightens casement, sill, and wall
Brighter light herself bestows,
　　Gladd'ning, quick'ning, conq'ring all ;
Phœbus' self doth dull appear
Set in list with sweet Rahere !

Night winds whisper, soft and low,
   All about her virgin nest ;
Zephyr wings that, waving slow,
   Lull her, soothe her into rest ;
Sweet their fall, yet rude and drear
Matched with tones of sweet Rahere !

Scents from herbs and flow'rs distilled—
   Perfume meet for palaced kings—
Grateful rise ; the air is filled,
   'Tis as Araby had wings.
Rich are they, yet come not near
Saba's empress, sweet Rahere !

Waken, then, my life, my queen,
   List thy lover's serenade ;
Love is life, there's naught between :
   Wealth is burden, pleasures fade.
Waken ! show nor fault nor fear ;
Bid me worship, sweet Rahere !

Thus sang the unseen minstrel.   While Rahere
Uncertain stood, half doubtful that she heard
Aright herself so lauded, and her name
So frequent sounded, knocking rose without
The further archway of the gate, with call
Expostulant and angry :
                ' Master Gould !
Some godless gallant sings anigh the gate.
But now the son of Belial lift his voice
Within the yard.   Come down and let us in !'

This loud, then softer, nearer, underneath
Her very casement : ' Prithee, get you gone,
Sir Edward, ere the crop-eared curs break in.
Away in haste ! you do the maiden wrong
If you but linger.   Get you to the inn !
Away, I say—away !   These canting knaves
I'll cozen smartly !   Go you, and good-night !'

She knew the voice, her host's.   An honest man—
Too honest to assume a godliness
As outer as the garments donned at morn
By them, alas ! too oft that most of all
Claimed nearer kinship with th' Inscrutable.
Too manly he to let unworthy strain,
Or treach'rous, rise about her couch at night ;
But rather had th' offender soundly trounced,
And chased afar the precincts of the gate.
Who, then, was he that sang beneath her pane,
And sang of love and passion ?
                                        Burning blush
O'erspread her cheeks.   'Tis very sweet to love,
But loved, how much the sweeter !   She was maid
And lonely.   Small the wonder now her heart
Throbbed with a sweet confusion, while her cheek
Flamed with the soft impulsion of her heart.

Her taper self-extinct, what time the song
Drew to an end, she turned her lattice catch,
And softly set ajar the leaden frame.
Beneath within the moonbeams' placid light
Her host stood restless, urgent—nigh him one
In whom she thought to recognise the youth

She met beside her namesake effigy.
Now grew the knocking louder.   One swift glance
Cast at her casement, and the youth was gone
With wafted kiss that seemed to her, sweet child !
To flush her burning cheek with deeper flame.
He gone, her host with quiet laughter flung
Aside his cap and jerkin, then in haste
Made for the knocking, while the maiden sought
The greater chamber, better so to hear.

Beneath there stood the watch with burning horn,
And halbert gleaming in the ashen light ;
With him two stern-faced burgesses returned
From business, doubtless, of a godly sort.
To them if 'twere not nasal psalm, a song
Was grievous and offence to Christian ears ;
So heard they scandalized the serenade,
But, as kind Fortune willed it, too far off
To catch its purport.   Calling quick the watch
From shelter corner, came they to the gate.

'What would you, watch ?' now queried honest Gould,
Unbarring slow the gate.   'Your noisy staff
Makes such a clatter, sure my harmless gate
Will need fresh paint the morrow.   Pray you cease.
Your worships' pardon !'—this to burgesses,
The door ajar : 'I knew not who did knock.
Methinks, indeed, the business must be great
That keeps so late our aldermen afoot,
All honest folk asleep.   But never shoe
I hammer after dark for mayor or cit.'
Impatient now made answer one : 'You do

But hinder matters, Master Matthew Gould;
Some ale-house tippler lurks within the yard,
Singing his lewd and godless melodies.'
'Art sure? art sure?' the farrier made reply;
'Come in then, friends! And but your worships catch
The roister knave, my stave shall play a tune
About his back; he'll wake no more o' nights
His brother citizens from honest sleep.
Come in, and quick! Why, what is that?   Good lack,
I fear 'tis truth!   There goes the villain!   See!
Your lamp, good watch! This way! This way, and quick!'

Within the further corner, where the gate
Threw blackest shadow, set a little down
Below the cobble paving of the yard,
A muck-heap, partly emptied, lay concealed;
Some soilage yet was left, and, foul and black,
Came level with the yard.   This way ran Gould
Beside the rest, but, stumbling as he ran,
Put out the light.   The rest went eager on,
With cry vexatious, changed to shout of wrath,
What time the foremost fell within the pool,
And clutching as he fell pulled all within!

Now came the farrier.   'Why, my masters, why,
And didst not see the path!   Phew, phew! the stench!
There! there!   The rascal's 'scaping at the gate;
I'll after!   Pray you home and shift your hose!'
They, well bemired, got out, and full of rage
Made home in haste.   Short time the watchman stayed
To light his lamp; then, cursing meddling fools,
Went off enraged, while stifled laughter shook
The fence where Gould in darkness hid away.

IV.

Next morn Rahere, at foot of oaken stair,
Perceived her host with purpose loitering near,
A merry twinkle lurking in his eye.
'Didst hear naught yester-eve, or rather night?'
He asked complaisant, laughing as he spake.
'We had some merry doings after dark
With music 'neath your window.   What didst hear?'

Then blushed Rahere, like ocean when the sun,
Unfolding slow at eve the western gate,
Departing casts a broader, ruddier gleam
O'er all the realm of water.   So the maid,
Confused, stood blushing, then made answer slow :
'In truth, I heard a song—a pretty song
With name ; yet, surely, 'twas not meant for me—
And at its end a knocking.   Then a shout
And splashing.   Then anext my very room
Such laughter as might shake the very gate.'

Here Gould again brake forth.   His laugh at end :
'Ay ! ay !   Indeed we choused the rascals well !
Yet, prithee, nothing say an you would keep
Myself, your friend, from mischief.   I am not
In wholesome odour with the livery ;
They know I ran not with the scurvy crew
That baited to his death our royal stag.
Your father was my friend, so am I yours,
And thereto bound the more that evil times
Depress your pretty head.   In truth, the song
Was somewhat, and for you.   I love the lad

Who sang it. 'Tis a goodly youth, whose heart
Is nobler fibred than a thousand—one
A queen might spouse without disparagement.
Some day he'll be Sir Edward—rarely rich—
Sir Edward Hewett, heir to great estates,
His crafty father kept or gained through all
The stormy years whose muttering's not yet past.
My brother has a stithy on the chace
At Hadley nigh the park.   Whene'er I may
I saddle Bess, and spend a healthful day
Amid old faces.
                    Thus it comes about
I know the lad full well—he me ; and should
He say a word of love to one I know—
Ay, blush your fill and welcome !—chide him not ;
But take Dame Fortune's proffered gift, and bless
The day the boy came wooing.'
                              All the morn
Rahere sat thoughtful, while her needle moved
More slowly than of wont.   But when the day
Drew evenward, her broidery set aside,
She went abroad within the Pancras fields
To cull a posy.
                    Soon her kirtle full
Of wildings plucked from hedge and bank and field ;
Germander, tutsan, balm of warrior wound,
White cuckoo-buds that, sootheful even come,
Gave out the sweets refused to fiercer day ;
With poppies, Flora's darlings frolicsome ;
And bindweeds pinky-veined, and sweet as gale
Of summer drowsed amid the hay-strawed fields.

All these and more she twined with ivy spray,
Resting awhile beside a little wood
Of hazel-bush and beeches. These the wind,
Awaking, shook, but softly. Gathering strength,
It sturdier blew, tree answering tree, till all
The wood rang loud with shout harmonious,
That swelled to tumult, then, subsiding, died
Away to very whisper. More removed,
A bell gave forth its monotone, and bade
The restful hamlet kneel in common prayer.

Soft was the maiden's heart, the peaceful spell
Of even laid upon her. Oft her spoil,
Her wilding spoil, she kissed with word of praise,
And some, prime-favoured, set within her breast.
A little while, and now the call to prayer
Rang out no more, its last stroke floating by
Reluctant, slow, and trem'lous. Overhead
The lark hung doubtful, songless; then began
Fresh ditty, fitful; then gave o'er, and sank
To turfy nest. The sun, with effort, clave
Apart the closing curtains of the west,
Once more to kiss the sorrowing face of earth.
Soft was the maiden's heart. Her fair face set
Towards the gleaming west, the crimson glow
Illumined cheek and throat, her wondrous eyes
Filled with the glorious radiance. Long she sat
Absorbed in virgin fancies, till the flame
Died out the purpling sky, and louder grew
Within the wood eve's wind-struck harmonies;
Then woke she smiling: 'Sith the sun is gone,

I too must homeward !' Yet a little while
She lingered still, as loathful to forego
Green wood and field, with gleamy eve, for town.
Again she lift her posy to her lips,
And softly sang a simple ditty, made
By one whose soul dwelt most with flowers and field.

> Flowers, flowers ! never shone
> Gems as fair on empress' breast !
> Hesper set in Evening's crest
> Never brighter ! Ye to me
> Dearer are than pearls of sea,
> Or chalcedone !
>
> Flowers, flowers ! seraph tears
> Are ye, shed for earth's despite,
> Rainbow-tinted in your flight
> Earthward, so that weary men,
> Hope-cheered, yet may climb again
> To loftier spheres !
>
> Flowers, flowers ! minster spires
> Are ye, glad with anthem, prayer,
> Heavenward lifting ! Spirits rare,
> Planting hope, uprooting doubt,
> Scornful chasing mammon rout
> With altar fires !
>
> Flowers, flowers ! sweet are ye,
> Yet but mirrorings of life,
> Portent emblems, warning rife ;
> Fair at morn, o'erblown at night
> Plucked to perish ere the light
> Unfailingly !

Her simple song at end, Rahere arose
And turned her footsteps homeward ; but confused
A moment after, let her posy fall.
A bridleway that crossed the beechen wood
Gave here upon the road, and by its gate
She saw the youth dismounted—him that moved
So late to pleasant dreaming. Eager he—
The falling flowers perceived—came quickly forth,
And set again the posy in her hand
With courteous salutation.

                She, sweet girl,
All trembling, blushing, took again the spoil ;
But never word could find to make reply,
Could only rev'rence. He embolden'd thus,
His horse's rein within his nervous hand,
Permission craved—the night so near—to guard
Her maiden footsteps homeward. This obtained,
A little way they went in silence, save
From time to time he spake her with his eyes,
Love's facund spokesmen. She within their depths
Read deep-set sadness, and, herself most sad,
Felt Love's kinswoman, Pity, stir her breast,
Forerunner oft of passion.

                    ' I am glad,'
He said at length—youth ardour daring tale—
' To meet you thus. The evening is so fair
And calm, mild thoughts must dwell in rudest breast
How much more then in her, whose loveliness,
Though perfect, yet doth hold but second place
To all the sweet impulsings of her soul !
Rahere, when first I saw thee in the church

So sad, so droopful, nigh the founder's tomb,
My heart sprang up tumultuous, while the blood
Burned in my veins, and all my being turned
To thee as needle turns to magnet stone.
Dear heart! dear heart! I prithee, show not cold,
Nor turn so far away that kindling face.
You deem me stranger—nay, not so! Long days
And weeks have gone since then—long dragging days—
But never once my thought has gone from thee.
Rahere! Rahere! believe me, day nor night
Has passed but I have sentinelled thy haunts,
Now church, now gate. Unseen, I oft have seen,
And seeing, loved but deeper. Yet whene'er
I drew anigh to speak thee, something rapt
The courage from my heart.
                               But yester-eve
Our common friend spake out, and bade me cease
Pursuit or plead. Rahere! dear trembling queen!
I love thee—love thee! Well I know thou art
As far above me in thy nobler self
As heav'n from earth. Yet as the sun beholds
Sin-troubled earth, and sends benignant beam
Incessant through untravelled space to cheer
Her tear-worn bosom, so behold me now,
And grant, of sweet compassion, love for love.'

So urged he ardent, letting fall the rein
He held, to take in his the maiden's hand.
She nothing spake as yet, the thoughts that stirred
Her breast too new, too strange, too various all
For utt'rance; only as he gazed, his face

Turned so to read her own, he saw the tears
Beflood her eyes, then fall, delightful pearls
Of hope to him enraptured.
                              Yet again
He spake, and truthful spake his very soul :
'Forgive me !   Never tear should stain those cheeks
Unless begot of love.   I speak, perchance,
Too soon, and vex you, yet can naught withdraw.
You are my first and only love !   If thus
Unpractised tongue in lover speech be rude,
O'erlook th' offence, and teach me how to woo.
Your pretty song I heard—I could but hear,
Your every tone to me a melody—
Recalling voice of her who gave me birth,
And sang, alas ! as cagèd lark, or swan
Just before death, of heart-break weariness
And very joy of dying.   List'ning, then,
To this your song, one only thought was mine :
Sweet singer, may I haply win thy love !
I'll wear thee, flower of maidenhood, more close
To warder breast than rose to stem, or bloom
To coronal of leaves, or ivy spray
To shelter wall, storm-shelt'ring still in turn.'

He urging nothing more, she slowly turned
Her lovely face—more lovely for the tears
Still glitt'ring on the fringes of her lids—
And answered gently : ' I am homely maid,
Priest's daughter only, and with only dower
Of comeliness, while you are rich and great.
How can it be you love me as you say,

And I so little seen—known scarce a day ?
But yet I may not wrong you as to doubt
Your pleading true.   Myself forbids the thought.
You plead as I had pleaded, were I you,
My heart so sad with weight of loneliness ;
And so in truth the proffer of your love
Doth sorely tempt.   Yet will I never wed
Unless my every thought is set on him
Who hails me bride with holy vow and kiss.
I may not seal love's sacrifice of self
But I can blend in ampler, worthier stream
The current of my being, wishes, hopes ;
Nor slave nor toy, but helpmate, comrade, friend,
To him, true image of the God that said,
" It is not good that man should be alone."
Let this content you, then, I'll be your friend ;
And if, as may be, friendship grow to love,
Then will I choose thee—all beside contemned —
For lover, husband, keeper of my soul,
While Heav'n doth sanction earthly wardenship.'

All overjoyed, again and yet again
Her yielding hand he lifted to his lips
With murmured blessing.   'Darling, soon I'll bud
Plain stock of friendship with the choicest bloom
Of life's wise gardener, love.   My queen, my own,
Erelong shall weight of loneliness be lost
In world of gain.   Nay, where is loneliness,
Dear heart, already ?   Look me, love, in face,
Read all my soul, with those so lustrous eyes,
And spurn me loathsome doth a single thought

Lurk in't against true love and constancy.
And now, beseech thee, give me pledge of thine—
A flower, thrice happy simple, to have sprung
And grown and bloomed and flaunted but for thee.'

From out the ivy twine she took a flower,
And, blushing, held it forth with modest face.
' Nay, now, Rahere—nay, now, I prithee ! this
Love-pining bloom that nestles in thy breast,
Sweet woodbine, fair Fidelity's own flower,
I'll keep it ever.'   Smiling, from her vest
She took the spray and set it in his hand ;
He, kissing, put it by.   But now the glow
Of sunset gone, the star of eve shone out
Full in their path.   Then said he thoughtfully,
The while they journeyed homeward : 'See, Rahere,
Yon golden orb that lights our darkening way ;
Shines it not fairer than of wont, as if
It smiled upon our compact ?   Ah ! how oft,
Dull-thoughted, have I stolen forth to seek
True comrady in Night's slow-circling fires !
There's oft deep speech in silence.   So to me
Their solemn stillness spake me through and through
With thrill of comfort, burning like the coal
That fired the prophet's lips to eloquence,
Beyond the power of mortal ecstasy.
Nor seldom 'neath their pain-assuageful ray
The void that ached my heart was wondrous filled
While all its hunger fled my solaced soul ;
But not of late.   Since I beheld thy face,
To me more bright than welkin star, more fair

Than yonder glowing sphere, Night's glitt'ring host
No more delight nor satisfy.   Alone
One star for me can gild life's firmament,
Or fill the crannies of my soul with light ;
And thou, Rahere, the star !'
                              Much more the youth
His tongue unloosed of love, poured in her ear,
She not unwilling list'ner.   He was such
To sight as maid might covet—comely, tall,
Gracious withal in mien, and in his speech
More lofty than of common.
                              Nearing now
The town, the gloom well-nigh to darkness grown,
A cheery voice accosting bade them stay.
Matt Gould it was, with cudgel staff, who drew
Athwart their path with merry laugh and quip.
' So, so !   I came to seek an errant maid,
But find my questing needless.   Younger swain
Hath found the truant damsel.   Pearls of price
Have eager seekers ever.   Give you both
Good-e'en, and bid you back with me to sup.
Now you, Sir Ned, have found your tongue, I gage
You prove the pasty scorned but over-night,
With rare amend for lover fast and fret.
But come you at your leisure.   By your leave
I'll ease you of your horse, and snug him down
Before you find the gate.   To-night shalt sing
Our pretty maid as oft and how thou wilt,
Nor care a fig for prowling presbyter.

V.

Day following day, week week, Rahere had come
To wish her lover's presence, and to watch
His coming out the window of the gate.
Not seldom rode he proudly through the square,
His gaze fast set upon the lattice broad,
With ever hope the gleamy glass might show
Benignant, fairer face than artist monk,
Saint visioned, e'er had burned in cloistral pane.

To-day so came he; saw her in her seat
From far, and, hast'ning, doffed his hat and smiled
Fond greeting upward, while his sparkling eyes
Drank at her beauty draught that, Tantalwise,
But fired his lover calenture the more.
The day was fine; the sun his brightest shafts
Rained at the gate and casement. Gaily fell
The golden rays about her as she stood
Beside the open lattice. Half apart,
Her pretty lips spake welcome—welcome writ
E'en in their parting. Far adown her hung
Her tressèd wealth of purpling black that caught
The ray, and gave back sheen for sheen, but yet
More softly, mildly. Light was in her eye,
The light of dawning love, fair wizard flame
That homeliness to comeliness transforms,
And comeliness to beauty, such as brings
To lips of good men blessing !
                                    Thus she stood,
To blush anon, her lover's gaze so long,
So deep, so ardent. Soon upon the stair

She heard his hurrying footsteps.   Now her hands,
Quick seized, were lifted eager to his lips,
Nor this alone, for reading in her eyes
Awakening love, he clasped her to his breast,
And burning kisses rained on cheek and lip.

Ah, first embrace of honest passion! bliss ✦
Of love's first pæan beat in breasts, compressed
Each unto each with answering tumult thrill!
This now was theirs.   Rahere all trembling clung,
With never word, her lovely head against
His shoulder, so to hide her blushing face;
One arm about his neck, one hand fast locked
Within his own.   Then spake he joyously:
' Rahere, Rahere! my lady and my life,
Thou lovest!   Ah, the joy that fills me now!
Yet, yet, I knew thou couldst not choose but own
Full soon life's talisman young love for lord!
Look up, dear heart, look up!   Waste not the light
Of those bright eyes upon the churlish ground;
But let me read them, sweet, as now, and see
The haven of my hopes deep set within
Their tearful lustre.   Darling, lift again
Those cherry lips, so I may seal them up
With kisses numberless as drops of rain
That fresh the parching fallows!   Love, my love!'

Thus he, enraptured.   Lifting up her head,
One glance she gave him, trustful, joyous; then
More closely nestling to his breast, like dove
In nest at eve beside her trusty mate,

Lay restful, peaceful, while he spake again :
'So lie then, love, so lie ! none other maid
E'er lay there, or shall lie, but only thee !'
So thus awhile.   Then softly urged Rahere,
What time she drew, but gently, from his clasp :
' My heart so full of happiness, I grow,
I fear me, selfish !   See, the day is fine,
And I did promise late Cecile, to spend,
If so might be, a space with her alone.
I wrote her so, what time you said Delight
Could, pillioned, bear me thither.   Let us go
To-day, and soon.   I long again to feel
The clinging clasping of her pretty arms
About my neck, her kisses on my lips,
To see the flushing deepen on her cheek,
And all her heart's love show within her eyes.
Mine, Edward, are but dull with hers compared ;
You call me fair, and praise me all too oft,
Yet am I glad, if so I am for you ;
But she indeed is lovely—never child
So fair in all great London—and as good
As beautiful !   Cecile, my pet, Cecile !'

Her lover smiled.   ' Most wondrous prodigy
She then must be.   I cannot fashion aught
More fair than thee, Rahere.   But whether fair
Or fairer, shalt thou see her, and to-day.
Delight shall have such burthen as before
She never knew, and prove herself well named ;
Gould has the pillion all in readiness.
Go, get thee ready, sweet !   But first the things

Cecile shall erelong give thee, give to me ;
I, too, love kisses, with the clasp of arms,
Cheek-flushing, and the light of loving eyes.'

What could Rahere but yield them ?   So again
The youth was blest, till callous Time—that recks
Nothing of love's sweet hunger, or the thirst
Of youthful passion—through the turret chime
Gave warning of his going.   Then with sigh
The youth gave up his darling, and withdrew
To see his horse caparisoned ; Rahere
To lave, not loath, her burning cheek, and lull
The tumult of her bosom, while she made
Her simple preparations for her ride.

Not long, and busy London left behind,
They came to Copenhagen in the field,
And thence to Highgate, where they stayed, first climbed
Its overhanging hill.   From thence again
To Finchley, often idling by the way.
The mid-day beam was hot, but welcome gale
Came from the north, and freshed them as they rode
Beneath the kindly canopy of boughs
That overhung the winding lanes they sought,
The rather than the sultry royal way.
Now leafy Tott'ridge showed, and now the farm
Which gave Cecile asile.   Beside a gate
And barn, a short way from the sheltered farm,
The youth drew up as bade Rahere, and soon
His trembling comrade set upon the ground.

'Your friends to me are strangers, but my name,
So well known hereabouts, would make me friend,
If but 'twere told.' Thus had the youth replied,
Rahere exhorting to avoid the porch.
Now stood he wistful by. 'Your wish is law,
Sweet love, to me, so fare thee well awhile.
Yet deem not I do fear to own thee, or
Present thee proudly all the kingdom o'er,
As Edward Hewett's promised bride and wife;
But be it as thou wilt. I'll come at eve!
Now get thee in, and quick. I go not hence
Till I have seen thee sheltered.'
                                    One fond look
She gave him of her love and gratitude,
Then hasty sped along the lane, and oped
The gate that swung upon the homestead lawn.

A pretty place it was, all overhung
With jessamine and clematis, and rose
That, higher climbing, cluster-blossoms laid
About the trellised wall. The house was old
And low, but spacious, built of rubble flint
With interlacing timbers. In the porch
Were seats amid o'ergrowing green, and here
Cecile sat reading. O'er the close-cropped lawn
Rahere impatient came, unheard, unseen;
Then halting, all her vision dimmed by tears,
'Cecile!' called softly. Startled at the sound
Of voice so loved, so longed for, all amazed,
The child let fall the book, then, springing up,
Sped arrowswift within her sister's arms.

'Rahere! Rahere!' she cried; 'Rahere! Rahere!'
Nor more could utter, save the much-loved name;
But kissing clung, and clung as she would grow,
Like ivy to the oak that parted dies.
What lover meeting e'er so purely sweet
As theirs, fond sisters? Angels both for gift
Of beauty, both for purity and power
Of loving, stood they love-enlocked, their tears
And sighs commingling. First Cecile found speech---
But broken, blent with sobbing, kissing, strain
Of circling arms, and beat of bursting heart—
'Rahere! Rahere! Then, then, 'twas but a dream.'
Then sudden brake away towards the house
With eager cry, that waked the leafy walls:
'Rahere is come! Rahere is come! Rahere!'

Now came there forth a pleasant country dame,
Who stilled the child, but not unkindly; while
She gave her hand in greeting to Rahere:
'Right welcome, niece! I would 'twere mine to say
My daughter, as for this young mistress here!
So did I urge, but William said me nay—
The younger only. Yet but come you in,
He'll greet you gladly, should he rathe return
From Barnet market.'
                              So Rahere went in,
Cecile still clinging, while the good dame smiled,
And chid her fondly: 'Wanton, well for you
I scorn jade Jealousy.'. Then to Rahere:
'She busses me at morning and at eve,
But never oft'ner. Well, the day may be

She'll serve me better. Truth, I'm glad to see
How much she loves you, for I thought her cold.
Come hither, wench, and give me, too, a kiss !
So, so ! `Now show your sister where you sleep ;
'Twill ease her heart to know you cosy laid.
Then go you round the garden and the moat ;
My pans need skimming, and my churning waits.'

With tearful joy Cecile led up the stair
Of rough but hearty oak, to where she lay ;
A pretty room, with curtains white as snow,
It was, with bed that smelled of lavender,
Meet for a queen, so freshly white and sweet,
Anigh a dormer window, where a spray
Of vagrant rose full oft impatient tapped,
As eagerly entreating to be in.
Well pleased Rahere beheld each sign of ease
And loving care, then earnest spake Cecile :
'Our kinsfolk love you. I am glad—so glad !
And you must love them, only not forget
Rahere, but name her ever in the prayers
She sometime taught you.'
                              At the words Cecile
Brake into weeping : ' Night and day, Rahere,
I see you, speak you ! Ah, were you but here,
How happy were we ! Yes, they love me ! Oft
I wake o' nights, a light within the room,
To see our aunt beside me. She doth pass
My chamber to her own, and ever looks
Within at passing. But to me no voice
Is, sister, as your own ; no touch so soft,

And yet so easeful ; and no kiss so sweet.
I wake, and waking miss them in the night.
But now I vex you.   Darling, do not weep !
No more of me, but tell me how you fare
At home, our home—ah me ! so far away !
So far !   Dost know when first I came, o' nights
I could not sleep for weeping—could not live,
Methought, without you ; so one noon I stole
Without the gate, and took the Hendon lane
To London, heark'ning ever for the bells
To ring, and cheer me as Sir Whittington.
But ne'er the bells did ring, and weary, late,
I sat beneath the hedge to rest, and fell
To sleep, and slept till startled by the rush
Of horse-hoofs by me.   Then I fearful woke,
To know the moon bright shining, and dismayed
Called out alarmful.   Then came back the horse
Full speed, and stopped beside me, while a man
Leapt off and clasped me : " God be praised !" he said,
And so I had no terror, glad to find
'Twas uncle.   Then he kissed me.   '' Silly child,
Your aunt is well-nigh frantic !   Come you home !"'

Amazed Rahere had never word.   Cecile
Went prattling on, half tearful, half ashamed :
' It was most foolish business, was it not ?
They said so, and I promised ne'er again
To go beyond the orchard or the croft.
But now come see the garden.   One broad bed
Is all my own, I grow whate'er I choose ;
But mostly marigolds, because, Rahere,
One day you said you loved them best of all.'

And seated in the orchard, on a bench,
Beneath a mossy apple-tree, whose fruit
Began to show the wooing of the sun
In tell-tale blushing, all her care forgot,
Who joyous as Cecilia?
                              In her hand
Was tire of ivy, tinct with marigolds,
And daisies deftly plaited, chaplet gay
Wove for Rahere, and set upon her head,
With happy laughter and long lingering kiss.

But yet again Cecilia, prattling, woke
Unwonted chords within her sister's breast :
'Last night, Rahere, I dreamed—of whom but you ?
A pretty dream, and yet 'twas cruel too !
I saw you in a garden, fairer far
Than any I have seen, or think to see,
So large it seemed to know no bounding, nor
Precinct of wall nor girdling thicket hedge,
But only hills of azure set with trees,
So tall they seemed to bear the clouds atop.
Oh, lovely was the garden !   I could bear
But hardly all the glitter and the sheen
Of flower and fruit and glossy leafiness !
And you were there, so beautiful, the tears
Sprang to mine eyes for very pride of joy—
All clad in white as bride to some great lord,
With crown as queen, and in your hand a bough
Of some fair tree.   But, ah ! your lovely face !
I saw the crown, the bough, the bridal gown,
But all were naught comparèd with your face.

Oh, never face beside was half so sweet,
So calm, so grave, but yet with winsome smile !
And in your eyes a marv'lous light, more clear
Than star, with never dazzling of the sun.
And as I looked I saw you lay your hand
Upon your heart, and, lo ! there sprang to view
Three names writ large.   The first, Rahere, was God ;
The next, Cecile ; the next—but now your hand
You took away, and sudden with mine own
The letters mingled, so I read them not.
Then called I out, " Rahere !" and strove to come
Whither you stood, but now for first perceived
A darksome river churning at my feet,
With waters deep and dreadful.   Then I wept,
And, weeping, stretched my hands across the stream ;
But then you lift the tree bough in your hand,
And smiled, and all the sorrow fled my heart.
" A little while—a little while, Cecile,"
I heard within me, yet you nothing spake.
And now most lovely music filled the air,
While all the garden faded from my view
With you, but you the last of all ; and then
I waked, a lark loud singing overhead,
And all my chamber full of melody,
The lattice left ajar.   Now, wast not strange
I thus should dream of you, Rahere, and thus
The morning of your coming ?'
                              Softly now
Rahere made answer, gazing fondly down
Into her sister's sparkling, quest'ning eyes :
' 'Twas strange indeed, Cecilia.   I did hear

Our father, once discoursing upon dreams,
Say thus : " It oft in olden days hath pleased
The mighty Lord, in visions of the night,
When deep sleep falleth on the sons of men,
To speak them for their profit. Joseph drew
To greatness thus, and Daniel. Yet more near,
Warned by a dream, the wise men crafty turned
Their faces homeward by another way,
Bemocking Herod ; while the manger cratch
Was emptied of its burden, and by dream !"

' To this did one make answer : " Yea, but still
The Preacher hath left record, ' Dreams do come
From multitude of business,' and the seer
Of Horeb bids his people put away
Dream-dreamers from their midst."
                                        No more I heard,
For then came one and called me forth, and thus
The gist and ending of their argument
I lost, but think our father had the right.
So may your dream be portent, shadowing joy
For me, Cecile ; or be but phantasy
Of often thought, with naught but prettiness
For aim and ending.'
                            Thus replied Rahere
With air serene, but yet was greatly stirred ;
She knew not why, and inly felt a thrill
Of mordant apprehension pulse her heart.

    *   *   *   *   *

Too soon, alas ! eve trod in track of day ;
Too soon the sunset shadowings creeping stole

Across the meads, and clutched the broader fields.
Too soon the molten glories of the west
Paled out, the sable ancient of old Night
Hung in the east, where argent Lucifer
Burst from the purple glooming, and his ray
Lent to his darkening sister of the skies.
Now came the pain of parting.   At the gate
Delight stood patient, while Cecilia clung
About Rahere.   ' Come soon again, Rahere ;
Come soon and tell me all.   You something hide ;
Your face is changed, but wherein cozens quest !
Your eyes have other deeper light than wont.
And now at hearing summons at the gate,
Your look lit wondrous.   Tell me, who is he,
This gentle ?   Nay, " next time " may never be,
Rahere, sweet sister !'
                              ' Patience still awhile,'
Rahere made answer ; ' and of this be sure,
Whate'er may be, my love for thee will ne'er
Grow less, but greater.   All my heartstrings twined
About thee, sister, never thought have I,
Or dream, or hope, but thou hast part, my own.
These kisses seal the compact—these again.
Now get thee in, and trust me all in all.'

Now rode the lovers home, and as they rode
Night slowly lift her jewelled coronet
Up to her brows, and reigned benignant queen ;
While secretly soft dews, uprising, bathed
Earth's sweltered face with drops narcotic, sweet
As Eastern maidens pour for couch of kings.

Again they took the less-frequented way,
But faster and in silence, till the youth,
As now they slower climbed a coppiced hill,
His mistress' hand took gently into his
With sportive question.
                    'Why so silent, love?
Hast fear, the road so lonesome, and the night—
But yet as night should be—so still and calm,
Delight doth tale our coming all abroad
With facund hoof-beat?   Sweet, there's naught to fear.
Give Parliament its due : the roads are safe,
And safer nearer to her seat and ken;
Short shrift, swift justice, make our footpads few.'
Then answer made Rahere : ' No night to me
Is other than the day.   Though sunny beam
Departeth for awhile, yet never He,
Light's Dayspring, shining ever more and more
About the paths of them that love Him, till
The perfect day.'
                    He silent ; spake again
Rahere in thoughtful accents : ' I am sad,
And know not why, yet sad with weight of ill
Implacable, impendent.   Surely he
Did write the truth and wisely, he that said,
" No joy so great but runneth to an end."
Who glad as I at morning and at noon?
Who duller now?   I can but think we stand
For ever girt about with essences,
Invisible but subtle, that do move
Our souls this way and that—good hap or ill
Our portion in life's keeping—biding time

For friendly admonition.'   Thus Rahere.
Then calmly spake her lover, while he kissed
Her clasping hand :
                    ' Sweet love, the damps of eve,
Dispelling now the fever heats of day,
Do press thee hardly.   I, too, had been sad,
But that my queen doth banish dumpish thought
With voice and presence.   Let us faster go,   ·
So shall the life-blood flush thy gelid veins
Again to gladness.'
                    Quickening pace, erelong
They reached a lonesome graveyard, that by day
Rahere had viewed complacent, as a spot
Where toil-worn pilgrims might disturbless rest,
So peaceful was it mid overhanging trees.
But here the youth turned quickly : ' Look afar,
Rahere, afar !   Look not within the garth.
Another way, dear heart, but never this !'
So said, and cast about his mistress' form
Protective lover arm.
                    The shadowy croft
A goodly space behind, ' What didst thou see,
Dear Edward ?' asked Rahere, low whispering.
' Why, nothing, sweet ; 'twas but in dread for thee.'
Thus he evasive.   So again she spake :
' Nay, tell me, Edward—tell me what didst see ?'
' Nay, love, 'twas naught.'   Now chid Rahere, but not
Ungently : ' Edward, surely thou didst see,
What I perceived before thou criedst out,
Corpse candle set upon a brambled mound.
'Tis sign of ill—death-presage !   Grant for me
The rather than for thee !'

'Now God forbid
The omen !' cried her lover—'yet 'twas so.
I would have hid the matter. Why didst see,
Rahere, the portent? Jesu ward the ill,
If ill depend, from my sweet mistress' head !'

VI.

At Beech Hill, in the park, beside the stream—
That, winding gently through the shelving meads,
Was now but eddying brook with grassy marge
And bed of glistening gravel, but anon,
Where Art, perfecting Nature, skilful drew
Apart its sinuous banks, was pretty lake
Bosomed in woody knolls—young Hewett lay,
And thoughtful, heedless, gazed upon the scene.

'Twas sunset ! All the water burned as blood,
And all the wood gave back the ruddy gleam
Of gold-edged cloudlet floating in the sky,
Meet canopy for crimson-orbèd king
Weary of labour, like himself benign.
Soft from the grove came forth the cushat's note,
Fit interlude for lovers, with the purl
Of brook, and hum of bee, late lingering, loath
To leave his thymy banquet. Low the leaves—
Moved by the mild and grateful gale that Eve
Called from the lake's calm bosom to awake
The woodland into dirge for dying day—
'Gan murmur, as a thousand elfin harps,
Soft struck, a moment swelled to hearing, then
Sank into silence deeper for the strain.

The youth lay still—so still, from out a herd
Of fallow deer a buck came cautious forth
To view him, doubtful ; while above his head,
Like arrowy streak of blue, kingfisher flashed,
And snatched from out the pool his quivering meal.
Unheedful of him, harmless, all about
The conies browsed the sward ; a royal swan
Came lazy floating out the islet's shade,
A little while to wait th' expected call,
Then sail indignant by.   But nothing saw
The lad of swan or cony, bird or deer,
His thoughts with his sweet mistress.   Did she roam
Afield amid the flowers, scarce as fair
And sweet as she ?   Or did her beauteous face
Show at her casement, 'neath the shade and guard
Of mailèd knight ?   Her thoughts, were they of him
And of the promise he had made her late,
To speak his father and reveal their love ?

But much the youth mistrusting what should hap
His love's avowal, nothing yet had said.
' He'll show full wrathful, scheming, in his greed,
Fresh gain through me, rich-wedded, at his will.
Alas ! that lust of gold should never sate,
But greater grow with growth of mammon heap,
Faith, friendship, honour, charity, consumed
Like tinder in the furnace fire of greed !
I am his only son, his only child ;
Would God his craze, as some say, had indeed
Myself for source and centre !   Foolish souls !
And I were dead, his idol yet would be,

And keenlier worshipped, lest unwelcome thought
Should gnaw his soul with viper memories.

'But yet he must be told. Rahere, dear heart,
Should no entreaty move him, as of me,
I'll bring thee suppliant to his gaze. Thy face,
Thy look, thy smile, sense-stealing eloquence,
Must surely move him howsoe'er his heart
Is warped to other.'
                         Thus the passioned youth,
Till sudden, in his musing, came a voice :
'I prithee, Master Edward, come anon ;
Sir Edward bids you to his presence. Come !'
An ancient servitor it was that spake,
Of lean and grizzled aspect, yet whose heart
Was young with honest love for him he bade
His father's chamber. So the lad arose.
' What now, good Gilbert ?' Slow the old man shook
His hoary head. 'Why, truly, naught that's kind
Methinks, dear lad. He frowns and fumes like wife
Late married and first thwarted. In his hand
He held a letter. Hast thou run in debt ?
Best break a limb i' faith than shake his purse ;
Whate'er it be, speak soft and bide thy time.'
The hall attained, an old and ivied pile,
Moated in part, and set upon a slope
With avenue of elms, loud voiced with call
Of restless rook, home-turned at close of eve,
The lad clomb slow the terrace steps, the tail
Low-trailed of lazy peacock barring way.

A little off Sir Edward glouting stood,
His tall, thin form erect, his eyes ablaze.

11

Not yet had age abased his stately head,
Though trace of winter rime was in his hair.
True father was he, of as comely son
In feature and in bearing.   Pity 'twas
Such goodly form could house such sordid soul !

In anger now : ' So, sirrah, you are slow
To come at bidding.   Nay, no words—a wench
'Twould seem can move you faster, thousand times !
I bade you to my closet.   Sirrah, in !'
Now flushed the youth's proud face, yet said he naught,
Thought of Rahere restraining sharp reply ;
But followed as his angry father bade
To inner chamber.   Here from out his vest
Sir Edward took a letter.   ' I am told,'
He said in tones of mingled rage and scorn,
' Herein that you have plighted troth with one
Whose only dower is comeliness and craft ;
Some sluttish outcome of a sluttish dam,
Yourself, were you your father's son, would scorn
To courtesy, still less to take in arm
But as the passing plaything of an hour.'

Much moved, the lad made answer : ' Sir, 'tis truth,
And yet 'tis not, the truth so foully hid
In slander lie !   The maid is angel pure ;
No slut, but one whose picture on these walls,
Save one, would dull all others.'
                                   Here the knight
Brake out sarcastic, while his steely eyes
Told louder of his anger than his tongue :
' So love-sick lout doth ever brag his wench.

Go ! give the girl a fairing, and have done.
There's naught in woman man may not attain,
From highest to the lowest, so he bid
But high enough—and naught that's worth the wage !'

The youth was noble, and a noble shame
Now filled his soul, and, rising, burned his cheek,
And flamed his sparkling eye.   'Sir Edward, he
That had Dame Ellinor Lestrange to wife
Should think far other thinking.   She I love,
Like her that sorrowing bore me to yourself,
No gift could cozen.   Were Golconda mine
Set at her feet, she'd spurn it scornful—loathe
The lecher tempter.'
                    Here Sir Edward laughed
A bitter laugh.   'Perchance to you, but not
To him her woman instincts follow soft
As spaniel after keeper.   Boy, there s naught
In life that's worth an hour's pursuit but wealth,
With that it bourgeons, wise engend'rer, power.
A word within thine ear.   Dost think for long
The nation will endure its present rule ?
Or that which bruited, next will follow on ?
The throne did topple down through tyranny
And tyranny shall set it up again,
But once the people cognizant of this,
Protector is but king, called otherwise.
I tell thee ere a year or two is gone,
The king will come again, while he that's rich
Will have the king in keeping.   You do think,
With many more, I worship gold as gold.

Now know me better.   Larger plan have I
For self, and so for you.   Enough of this,
And of your puling mistress.   As your heart
Is set on wiving, I have made approach
On your behalf.   My lord of Massinghurst,
Though poor, is high connexioned.   We are rich
And gentle born.   The girl is passing fair.
Once wedded, Hymen's sateful intercourse
Will bate your boyish fever otherwhere.'

Dismayed, the lad stood thoughtful, then began,
First doubtful, hesitant, thereafter firm :
' With deference, sir, I am of age to choose
My wife, and take her never other hand !
I love, and loving, plighted troth.   For great
And small alike, can be no greater shame
Than faith-pledge rudely broken.   I will wed
But only her I love, or rich or poor.'

Hot anger paled Sir Edward's face ; his tones
Were icy cold and slow, what time he made
Stern answer to his son's rebellious speech :
' Do nothing foolish, sirrah.   I will give
Thought ample time to gyve o'er-hasty speech.
To-morrow think it o'er.   Next day I'll take
Your answer, but be well advised.   No son
Are you if then your will encounter mine.
Your cousin shall inherit.   All my wealth
I will him, so he promise what I ask.
No words ! no words ! but do your father's will,
Or know you never more your father's son.
 Tis writ of Paul, " Children in everything

Obey your parents, and so please the Lord."
If then 'twas needed, much more now. The text
Should hang about the neck of every chit
That deems himself a wiser than his sire.'
Sir Edward ending, fain the youth had urged
Somewhat remonstrant. But more haughtily
The knight bade silence : ' Sirrah, get you gone !
Your duty is plain-portioned. Nay, no more !'

Dismissed, the lad long time beside the lake
Paced troubled and uncertain. Nothing he
Had of his own ; his mother's ample dower
Gone but to swell his father's store ; her kiss
And blessing all his heritage, at end
Her weary soul's unselfish pilgrimage.
What could he, driven forth his father's hall,
But sink to clod at home, or parasite,
Or mercenary to a friendly state
Abroad, or danger-vironed pioneer
In verdant Delaware, Connecticut,
Or fair Virginia, loyal last of all?

So all night long, with aching heart, the lad
Moved restless, ever in his ears the stern
And threatening accents of his angry sire ;
And ever tugging at his heart his love ;
And ever present, phantom of his thought,
Rahere's fair face, and love-compelling eyes,
For heart-ache comrade of his harass watch.
Day brake, and then, outwearied, lay he down
Awhile within his chamber. But his sleep
Was fitful, broken, aye-returning thought
With each awakening bringing deeper pain.

VII.

Slow wore the morn away, to him an age ;
And lingering noon gone by, he rode Delight
To London, there again to meet Rahere.
'Twas now her custom nigh the little wood
To wait her lover's coming.   Then at end
Their greetings, would she lay her gentle head
Upon Delight's soft mane, and pat his neck
With word of proud endearment, while the horse
Would paw the ground impatient, glad
Again to bear the fairest mistress e'er
His kind did burthen !
                          So to-day she stood
A little off the copse, within the way,
A chaplet hanging from her hand, her eyes
Lustrous with joy that daily grew to more.
Half proud, half shy, with diffidence of love,
She stood sweet vision, never more from out
His anguished heart to vanish.   Stood fair maid,
Her cheeks, like summer roses flushed at eve,
With deeper ruddier radiance ; while her long
Dark tresses let adown—for so he loved—
Hung graceful all about her virgin dress
Of snow-white cam'lot.   Ah, so fair, so pure,
So winsome was she, that the tears, all night
Kept back of manly shame, now sudden filled
His eager eyes, and in his heart he cried :
' My love ! my love ! Rahere, mine only love !
And must I give thee up at callous call
Of miser father !'   Sighing drew he rein,

Apale with deep emotion. She in haste
Sprang to his side : ' Dear heart, how pale your face !
Your eyes are dulled ! Your hands are deathly cold !
You tremble, Edward ! Tell me, all is well ?'

So said she troubled, all the summer blood
Departing from her cheeks, as swift she set
His hand against her lips, while answering tears
Shone in her eyes, like dewdrops flushed of morn.
Quick, bending in his seat, he kissed the lips,
And eyes so oft entreating : ' Nay, 'tis naught ;
Come mount you up, my queen ! A little way.'
· Nay, stay you here, my Edward. You are wan.
Come sit within the wood. Yon ivy bank,
With droop of ashen bough for canopy,
Doth proffer welcome seat.' Within the wood
Thus urged, he slowly rode, and then Delight
Made fast to nether bough, they sat them down.
' Now tell me all your trouble. Do not hide
A thought, of thought to lessen aught for me.
I am affliction's daughter. Tell me all !'
So said she bravely, combating the dread
That chilled her, and for all she fought it down.

Soon all was told. Then sank her lovely head
Upon his heaving bosom. Sighing deep,
She lay there long, rapt haven of her hopes,
Then spake him trem'lous, sorrow making still
More musical than wont her silvery tones :
' He is your father, Edward. Oh, my love,
He is your father !' Then again was still,
Save for the swift uplifting of her arm,

To clasp his bending neck, and draw his lips
Down to her fevered own.   Through all her frame
He felt the throbbing of her agony,
And murmured, what he knew not, of his love,
With hundred pretty names, and kisses hot
On cheek and lip and brow.
                              Now lift she up
Her tearful face, and spake him once again :
' He is your father, Edward.   Though it break
My heart, you must obey him.   Foolish I
To think a moment he would suffer you
Wed such an one as I !   There is no way,
But you must please him, and forget Rahere !'
Here cried her lover madly : ' Love, dear love !
You cannot love me truly, an you bid
Me wed another !'
                     Here she bitter sighed,
Then kissed the lips that spake such unkind word :
' Not love you, Edward !   I not love you !   I,
So lone that gift of honest love did seem
Like manna fall'n from heav'n !'   Again her head
Sank on his breast, again her trembling arms
Drew him the closer, while she murmured low :
' Yet once again, my darling, let me rest,
And nestle where I foolish thought to lie
Through years of untold bliss and happiness.'

Then made he fervid answer : ' Lie thou so,
Rahere, for ever !   All will I forego—
Name, home, and wealth, so only, sweet, not thee !'
She sighed, then turned, still resting on his breast,

But turned enough her mournful eyes might see
The face of him she loved so well and true :
' Nay, Edward, nay ! Yet do I thank thee, love,
For such great proffer none but noble heart
Could proffer simple maid ! It must not be !
But now thou saidst I did not love thee true ;
In truth, I did not, could not, did I take
Such sacrifice at these dear clasping hands !
Disheired, and all for me. No, no ! and yet
How can I let thee go, and live my life,
Made duller thousand-fold for glimpse of light,
Grateful as sunbeam blessing dungeon cell !
Ah me ! ah me ! and yet what must be, must !
For thee, dear heart, your sire's enforcèd will ;
For me, more patient bearing of the cross
The Father of all mercies lays on me,
With this for comfort ever in my heart :
I have been loved—perchance am still—where'er
Fate drives me, and my darling, far removed.'

So said she, pitiless to self, her thought
Alone for him, for whom her lonesome soul
Yearned with a love unspeakable ; so bleak,
So cold, so dreary, life without him now !
He, groaning, strained her closer to his breast,
Urged by her love to render all for love,
But did not, dreading Fortune's hidden store,
So kept him silent. Sigh for sigh they gave
Long time, with lips that met in lingering kiss,
Till length'ning shadowings filled the murm'ring wood,
And the low sun began to farewell earth.

Then drew Rahere away.   'Farewell ! farewell !
Oh, woe is me, that I must say the word !
But yet it must be spoken.   Edward, kiss
Me once again !   Be happy !   Do not fret
With thought of me ; but if thou canst, forget.
Farewell ! thou'st far to ride.   Poor, poor Delight !'

A kiss she set upon the horse's neck,
Then swiftly moved away with streaming eyes.
Far better thus that she had gone ; but now,
Moved by the lover tempest in his soul,
He sprang her after, clasped her, turned again
Her wistful face towards him, passionate ;
Then spake in quick and bated breath : 'Rahere !
There is a way, himself did urge it.   I——'
But here he faltered, trembling, and with shame,
Nor dared to meet her virgin gaze, but cast
His burning eyeballs earthward.   'Oh, my love,
'Twere death to me with other, living death !
We must not part.   Rahere ! Rahere ! of old
Men after His own heart, who planted love
Deep in our own for endlessness of life,
Had wives, and others, wives in all but name.'

Here faltered he again, while she, amazed,
Heard and not heard for anguish thrill of shame.
He moved anew from madness of his love
To speech, and out her silence snatching hope,
Perceiving not 'twas horror held her lips,
Spake wildly :
                    'Rachel only was beloved,
And yet was Leah wife to Jacob too.
He sinned not, spousing both.   Rahere ! Rahere !'

Her arms fell slow from off his traitor neck,
As from his grasp she drew her slow away.
One mournful look she gave him, as he stood
Confused, nor daring to behold her face.
No word she spake, no tear she shed, no moan
Brake from her breaking heart, but slow away
She moved as one in dream with aimless tread.
A little space she went, then turned again,
Came swiftly back to snatch his listless hand
And press it to her lips, her quivering lips ;
Then spake as one that speaks from o'er the grave :
' God bless thee, Edward, darling !   I forgive !'

He let her go, scarce knowing what he did ;
His mad eyes blurred with hot and blistering tears,
His brain awhirl, his heart with tumult throb
Anear to bursting forth its fleshly cell.
He let her go.   Ah, God ! that shame could hold
Him so fast bonded that he made no sign—
Could speak no word—could only see her go
In agony of silence, misery, shame !
He let her go—Rahere, dear child of woe !
Her hands fast clasped, her weeping eyes upturned
To that far home of many mansions—His
Whose love alone was left her, earthly love,
So soon to gall within her virgin soul,
Turned to her desolation.
                 Thus she went,
But not alone, for out aerial height
Came, at the cry that rived her stricken heart,
A sister-spirit, mild, compassionate,

Unseen, but not unfelt, whose angel hand
Touched heart and brain and heav'n-imploring eyes,
And bade the fountain of her crystal tears
Flow, and relieve her overburdened soul.

VIII.

Within her gateway chamber sat Rahere,
As Niobe distract, her children slain,
Fair progeny, late born of virgin dream
Of holy wedlock, honest spousal joy.
Upon her lap there lay an ancient book
Of prayers and litanies, by one who sealed
His faith in fiery torments in the days
That Spanish Philip wrought the land annoy.

'Twas midnight, and her taper, overhung
With fateful winding-sheet, and guttering low,
Told of the wakeful misery that held
Her gentle spirit captive, and repelled
Still-footed Sleep and poppy-winged Repose.
Ah, mournful was her face, as one that sees,
Spell-bound, the labour of his life destroyed ;
Nor voice can raise, nor hand can lift to save.
With weeping dulled, her piteous eyes the page
Scanned as with hope of comfort ; but no help
Drew from the collect, quaint initialled, nor
The pious meditation, earnest conned
By buried generations.   Still as death,
Droop-headed sat she long time ; then she sighed,
And, sighing, shut the book.

'My heart is dead
Within me.   Ah, forgive me if I sin,
Great Lord of all, for that I cannot say
As yet, "Thy will be done!"   So deeply set
Within our hearts the roots of mortal love,
Uptorn, we groaning perish !   Edward, love,
How couldst thou harbour such ungentle thought
Against me helpless ?'
                              Rising up in haste,
She trod the cell impatient, then resought
The larger chamber, where so oft of late
She watched her lover's coming.   Still the night
And warm, and so the casement stood ajar.
The moon was in her crescent, rising late,
And thus gave little radiance, yet enough
To fright the gloom and glint the warrior mail,
And life the time-old portraits on the wall.

Beneath the glimmering panoply she sat,
And laid her aching brow upon the cold
And dinted corselet of the monkish knight.
There sat she drowsed with sorrow, till disturbed
By lazy call of watchman, sleepy ears
Disquieting with tidings of the night.
Then woke again sad memory to sting
Anew her heart.   'Ah me, my love, my life !
In fancy I did set thee up so high,
Man-angel sent of heav'n to comrade me,
So desolate, love-hungry, lonely, sad ;
And thou wouldst thrust me down to concubine !
Ah, villain thought, to stain such lofty soul !

My lord—my one time Edward—false to name,
To me, to honour, and thy worthier self,
I love thee still—I love thee! God forgive
Me now for loving—honour bidding hate.
But that I cannot. Thou, too, lov'st the men
Thou madest, howsoe'er Thou hatest sin ;
And I am but a woman, made for him
And of him, lest his Eden Paradise
Should desert prove untrod of wifely mate.'

Again she laid her head upon the mail,
Again the piteous silence of the night
Gave back her sighs, returned her moan for moan
Till once again—a prayer upon her lips
For him—she, overborne, unquiet slept.

And sleeping—so did seem to her—a face
Fair as her own, but calm with mighty peace,
Did smile upon her ; while her being thrilled
With voice whose accents naught might intercept
Ethereal or material, yet were sweet
And musical withal as woodland rill :
'A little while, a little while, Rahere,
And churlish woe is janitor to bliss !
Weep, then, no more. E'en now cloud messengers,
Moved by His will, who worketh good of ill,
Do gather—latent in their sulphurous womb
New birth for thee, that evermore shalt joy.'

    *   *   *   *   *

Meanwhile her lover, equal in his pain,
With added sting of guilty shame, night long

Trod anguished up and down the dewy mead
For ever in his heart remorse; and aye,
Rahere, as last he saw her, in his brain;
And ever in his ears her last, last words:
'God bless thee, Edward, darling! I forgive!

Dear God! what scorpion whips we knot, who yield
Ourselves to devil-tempting and the lure
Of fever-flesh! What dragon crops of ill
Spring from our madsome sowing! Weary nights
Made sleepless of remembrance; agony
Of thought retributive; soul-madd'ning shades
Of deadly wrong; remorse unquenchable,
With goad of hell to lacerate the heart
Too late repentant! Woe of woes to feel
At length the curse of evil, and to know
We in our folly, selfish, heedless spread
The plague, and reckless heaped the pile of sin!
Nor less to know nor look nor word nor deed
Ours to recall, by prayer, repentance, tear!
The present ours alone, and what shall spring
From it, unknown, the future.
                              But the past!
Ah, God, the past! Thou keep'st it in Thine hand
Inviolate. We can but weeping fall
With pleading hands outstretched, and mournful cry,
'Undo for me—undo for me, dear Lord,
The wrong that haunts me! Kill the seeds of sin
I sometime sowed, lest in the day of doom
The harvest of my madness, mighty grown,
Press me to silence, self-condemned, and death.'

Most sad the youth ! The bitterest grief he knew
The livelong night. The wind compassionate,
Came fragrant from its journeyings o'er the meads
To kiss his brow and cool his fevered cheek ;
Then, laden with his sighing, stole away,
To spread the tale, meek sorrowing, through the chase.
Thus he outwatched the night. But when the Morn,
Gray-clad, her amber fingers at her lip,
Stole silent to the couch of slumbering Day,
And waked her virgin blushing, then resolve
Rose in his heart.

　　　　　　　' Now God forgive me, love—
E'en as thou prayedst—selfish thought unclean !
Farewell, dear home, if so must be. No more
I tread these pleasant paths ! Farewell, brave spot
Dear by a hundred recollections sweet
Of her that gave me being ! Mother, bless
Thine erring son ! That I should project ill
Against thee through another pure as thou !
Rahere ! Rahere ! heav'n's fair embodiment,
Gold against thee ! Most monstrous ! Love, ere Night
Again doth draw the curtains of the sky,
Laid at thy feet true penitent, I plead
Far otherwise, my queen, than yester-e'en !

IX.

Fair was the day, bemocking sorrowing heart
With gleam and sheen. No cloud beflecked the sky ;
The yellow sun poured down its beams undimmed,
And, upward soaring, drawing nigh to noon,
Flooded the face of earth with fruitful fire.

Sir Edward now bade fetch his son. The youth,
With pallid face but stern, obeyed the call,
And, silent, made obeisance.   Then the knight,
Loud-voiced and truculent, as one that reads
Resistance in the look of him he speaks,
And rudely would overbear it : ' Boy, the time
I gave you for reflection is at end ;
Your answer, and in brief.   You know me well—
Too well to doubt fulfilment of my threat :
Disheritance, or wedlock chos'n of me !'

Then urged the lad respectful : ' Sir, I fain—
With hope to move you yet to sympathy—
Would tell you first what chanced but yester-eve
Betwixt my love and me.'
                              ' Nay, never word !'
The knight returned, ungently and in haste ;
' Your answer and no more !'
                              Deep sighing now,
The youth made answer : ' Sir, I cannot do
Your will in this.   I dare not link my life
To one I love not—swear fidelity,
With ever lover-longing in my heart,
And passion for another.'
                              Now uprose
The knight, and drew him nearer : ' Yet again,
That none may say I moved in over-haste
Against you, though rebellious, yet my son,
I bid you think again.   You deem me rich,
And so I am, and yet and yet again !
None know but I what secret hoards are mine,

For all my gifts perforce to Parliament!
Has gold lost charm for youth? a pretty face,
Now white, now pink, as passion pales or burns,
More draws him, sottish, than the magnet wealth
That would allure a hundred to his feet
As beautiful as Phryne, or the slut
That havocked Ilium?   Answer me again!'

Again the lad's pale face flushed honest red,
As quick he answered, stern, contemptuous, cold :
'Wealth so employed were surely devil-chain,
Fiend-forged, to drag the debauchee to hell.
Perish the thought in me!   But yester-eve,
Bane-seed, of you implanted in my breast,
Upsprang to plant, that pois'nous fired my blood
To madness, and had sullied other too,
But for the Christ-given chastity that kept
Her spirit from pollution.   Sir, farewell!
You have my answer!'

                              'Ay, and you, sir, mine!'
Sir Edward cried in fury.   'Get you gone!
No longer son of mine, when I return,
Let me not find you hither!   Ere an hour
Is gone, Beech Hill, with all beside, shall pass
From you for ever!   Prater, get you gone!'

With heavy heart the lad withdrew, erelong
To see his father swiftly ride away
Towards Hadleigh and the scrivener's.   Then, o'ercome,
The hot tears seared his eyes, his voice was choked.
Old Gilbert coming soon with troubled face,
Part guessed, part known, the lad's distressful fate,

' Nay, Master Edward, say 'tis never true,'
The old man whimpered ; 'yet Sir Edward bade
Us never name you more.   Is gone in haste
To Scrivener Hurst at Hadleigh.   Bade us know
Henceforth for master after him, Sir Giles,
Your kinsman—sorry master he, God wot !
A lech'rous, brawling lad as ever wrecked
Estate, and trailed a goodly name in mire,
But turned of late to nasal saint and shrew.'

'''Tis true—too true, alas ! for me, old friend :
Sir Edward bade me that I could not do—
Be that enough—and so am cast adrift.
Now leave me ; come again an hour at end ;
Till then I fain would be alone.   Nay, go !
I must prepare me—must have space for thought.
You cannot aid me !'
                Left alone, the lad
Turned to the chamber where the portrait hung
Of her, his much-loved mother.   Silent here
He stood awhile, rapt gazing, as he ne'er
Might gaze his fill, then sadly spake : ' Sweet saint
And mother, have I done the thing thy lips
Had counselled ?   If so, speak me comfort now.
A little while and I am far away
From home and this thy living lineament ;
But thou, where'er thou joyest, look on me,
Soul of thy soul : my mother, send me peace !'

So for an hour the youth remained, now lost
In bitter thought and gloomy reverie ;
Now mournful, gazing upward at the face,

Whose parted lips seemed smiling fondly down,
As they would whisper, 'Patience, patience, child!
Bear thou thy cross, with God as arbiter
Of that thou doest, be it good or ill.'

'Farewell!' at length he murmured.   'In my heart
Thy face is burned as saint in minster glass.
Farewell!   Should passion tempt again, I'll turn
My riot fancy inward; cooling draught
Drink at those wells of angel purity,
Thine eyes, and out thy truth-imparting mouth
Draw wisdom, counsel, solace, and control.'
Thus he, then turned, but scarce a step, when hands
Were noisy laid against the fast'ned door,
While voices clamoured loudly:
                                            'Sir, come forth!
Come forth! his honour's nigh to gasp.   Come forth!'
In haste the bolt slid back ; he bid them cease
Their clamour—one to speak him, and for all.
Old Gilbert then : 'Sir Edward's horse had come
Again to hall, but riderless, so some
Had gone adown the avenue, to find
The knight upon the road in pool of blood!
'Twould seem he furious, heedless riding, fell,
And some way had been dragged.'
                                            With awful look
The youth received the tale : 'Chirurgeon one
Go fetch, and quick ; ride as for life!   Come not
Again without him !'   Then, 'Where is he now ?'
'Beside the walk.'   'Then some bring wattles, cloaks,
And cordials !'

Now beneath the arching elms
The lad ran swiftly. Nigh the Hadleigh lodge
His father lay unconscious. Kneeling down—
With horror at his heart, for that his thoughts
Had been so bitter 'gainst the stricken man,
However justly, yet his father still—
He took his senseless hand, and gripped it fast,
With frequent word of filial tenderness,
Compassion, and forgiveness.
                   Softly borne
Erelong to hall, and laid upon his bed,
Sir Edward, moaning grievous, woke to life,
To see the son, so lately spurned, o'erhang
His couch with gen'rous sorrow. Then a flush,
Quick mounting, fired his ashen cheek, as thought
Came back with mem'ry of his hate ; he turned
His battered head aside, and, frowning, groaned.

Small hope ! so went the murmur round the hall.
Chirurgeon aid obtained, the wise man's head
Shook ominous ; his scrutiny at end,
' His hours are o'er,' he whispered to the youth ;
' 'Twere best at once to send for minister.'
'Twas softly said, but yet Sir Edward heard,
And, careless smiling, made him faint reply :
' No need for leech to tell me I am sped.
Do you your best ; send not for minister.'

Soon all was done to comfort and assuage,
The while the knight, pain-swooned, lay deathly still.
Then sense returning, gazing round, he bade
All leave him for the present but his son.

Then spake Sir Edward feebly : ' Son, forgive
'Tis hand of God.   He would have turned me back.
I saw the Huntsman's spectre warning glide
Across my path, with pointing hand to hall,
But would not home, my heart so full of wrath.'
No more the wan lips proffered for a time,
Till, rousing up, the knight, with energy,
Spake for a moment, somewhat as of old :
' I do withdraw all thwarting !   Wed the maid,
And on you both my blessing.'
                              Here the youth,
All overjoyed, sprang up.   The wounded man
Smiled grimly : ' Son, be worthier spouse than I !
Too late I see true love doth outweigh gold.
Give me again the potion—quick, I faint !'

A little after : ' Bring me now my keys
From yonder escritoire.   See this, the least,
Doth ope a drawer within the nearer claw.
Go, bring me that thou findest—Ay, boy, ay !
'Tis well concealed—a key, and nothing else !
A little key !   Well, oft great things do spring
From small beginnings.   Turn you to the wall,
And mark the panel second from the hearth ;
Count now the acorns on the right ; the sixth
Unscrew.   Hast done it ?   Ay, a hidden lock.
That key doth fit it.   Hist ! I had forgot ;
First fast the door ; some knave might enter in.'

Exhausted now the knight lay breathing hard,
His son again beside him, holding still
The curious key that matched the panel lock.

His eyes unclosing soon, Sir Edward saw
The clef, and motioned eager to the wall :
' Go, open, and within,' he whispered ; so
The lad arose, and turned the key, to find
The panel, doorway, and beyond a space
Dim lighted, then an ancient orat'ry
Built in the wall, with loophole ivy-clad.

And going in, on every side was wealth,
The mow of years—gold harvest sprung, full oft,
From seed of neighbour need or indigence,
Watered with widows' tears, and mulched with shame,
Perchance, of maidens, sold for sustenance,
And ripèd with curses wrung from orphan hearts—
Reaped callous year by year, by him who now
Lay dying, and from out his royal store
Ease but an instant from his agony
Might never take—the dross untroubled still,
Though hell's worst pangs did rive its owner's soul.

Here parchments lay !   Here money-bags !   Here gauds
For neck and breast, with pendants ; these, too, laid
Of whim, or very recklessness of greed,
Upon the marble altar-slab, beneath
A broken crucifix, that still its place
Kept on the sordid wall.   A heavy sigh
Brake from the youth, astonished, gazing round :
' For this, and nought but this, a lifetime long,
How many a troubled heart this gold has broke !
How many might have solaced !'   Then the rood
He saw, and, all astounded, groaned.
                                            . ' Ah, Lord,

Better Thy pain and poverty and thorns,
Than ease and riches, all so ill attained !'

Now heard he once again his father's voice,
All feebly calling.   Quickly going back,
He closed the panel.   'Call you quick the leech,'
Sir Edward murmured.   So, the bolt withdrawn,
He fetched the man, who gravely shook his head.
'He has been talking overmuch ; 'twere best,
Indeed, he slept.   I'll mix him now a draught
Somniferous.'
        This given, erelong the knight
Sank into slumber stertorous, but first
Had prest his son's responsive hand and smiled.

'Now will he sleep long time !   Good sir, you look
As you, too, needed rest.   Go, lay you down !
He will not rouse till night.   I'll take your place.'
Thus the chirurgeon.   Then love-hunger woke
Within the lad : 'Art sure, Sir Andrew ?   Much
I fain would do within the next few hours,
If might be done without unkind neglect.'
'Canst safely do it.   Yet I'd urge thee sleep,
For fear mayst have to watch the livelong night.'

                         X.

Erelong Delight, caparisoned, in haste
Her ardent master bore along the road.
'Rahere ! Rahere ! now, love, to make amends
For Bedlam suit and tempting !   Ah, to throw
Myself at those dear feet, so lately turned
In such meek sorrow homeward, and from me !'

Fleet was Delight and eager, as she knew
Herself love's courier of joy to her,
Her sometime beauteous burthen. Fleet, but still
Snail-paced to him that rode her, chiding oft
The willing brute for laggardness, so fast
Impatient love outrunning steed in race.

But nearing town, clouds gathered ; and the sun,
O'ercast of scud and wrack—storm's harbinger—
Withheld his gleam. The lark gave o'er his song,
Disturbed, to seek the shelter of his nest ;
The cattle slow across the quivering field
Moved lowing to their covert. Soon afar
The cloud-heaped sky 'gan flashing, where it clad
Earth's dusky breast with pall of angry dun.
Now came the thunder, muttering low, and yet
Infrequent and slow-rolling.
                              At the sound
The youth looked back. ' Quick, now, Delight ; there's
        storm
A-brewing ! Quick ! and we escape it yet !'

So 'twas ; the gate was reached before the rain
Came down apace, though pattering drops presaged
The coming tempest, and made bare the streets.
The youth looked up. No face adorned the pane,
No form aneared the casement, though Delight,
As in th' unwonted stillness so did seem,
Gave forth more noisy tidings of approach.
In haste he led the horse within the yard,
Called forth the boy, and gave the brute in charge

Then questioned Gould, who also came at call :
' Where is she, friend? where is she ?   Tell me quick !
All's well—all's well ! Sir Edward gives consent.'
A light lit up the farrier's honest face :
' Good news is that, young master ! Something wrong
I thought betwixt you, surely, and the maid,
Who all night long was sorrowing, and to-day
Did naught but wander restless up and down,
Her work neglected, yet would nothing say,
Until an hour agone, upon the stair,
When Mary met her dressed for outer walk.'

' Yes, yes ; but tell me whither she has gone !'
The youth brake in impatient.   ' See, the rain
Begins to fall ; waste never time, but tell !'
' In church, then, will you find her.   She'll ne'er harm
Within its flinty walls from wind or rain.'
So Gould replied.   The lad, with lover haste,
His riding cloak drawn close about him, turned,
And up the lane, and o'er the martyr-field,
Made for the fane, through storm and plash and peal.

     *   *   *   *   *

Within the church, Rahere, more peaceful, knelt,
Her face less wan, her eyes less dimmed with tears ;
For felt she not again the comfort clasp
Of spirit arms ?   Again did she not hear
The echo voice of prayerful centuries
Persuade her softly : ' Daughter, pray.   Alone
In prayer is peace.   Pray thou for him and thee !'
Did she not kneel before the altar seat
Of Him whose presence age-long blessed the fane ?

Was not the tomb of him whose name she bore,
Himself with hands uplift in prayer, anear ?
Did not her mother sleep beneath the stone
Whereon she knelt, her father restful by ?

So slid into her heart the peace of God,
That passeth understanding—perfect peace,
Such as the world knows not, gives not—the peace
From Him proceeding who alone is peace,
And giveth of His bounty unto them,—
Pure souls, their pilgrimage approaching end—
That see in ecstasy the golden gates
And streets of Salem.
                          Thus the gathering storm
Did but in her, composed, awake the sense
Of fellowship with Him by whose consent
World elements do conflict.   Nigh the shrine
She knelt with eyes ecstatic ; on her lips
Low breathed prayer for him who even now
Stood at the porch, its brazen latch in hand.

      *   *   *   *   *

He entered, saw her meekly kneeling ; then,
The while his soul was full of lover joy,
The while her name did pulse upon his lips —
True penitent, with heartfelt word of love—
The flame leaped forth—a mighty flame that filled
The church, and ached his eyeballs with its glare.
Sight-blinded, all was blur, and mist, and daze ;
While the fierce thunder crashed, and rolled, and shook
The jarring casements every side, the piers,
For all their vastness, quivering at the shock.

Recovering, gazed he eagerly around.
Rahere lay prone. Was't fear ? was't shock ?   Alarmed,
He drew anigh, ' Rahere !' called softly, then
More loudly ; then ran forward, and upraised
The fallen maid.   ' Rahere, look up !   Rahere !'
Then, sudden, uttered loud and bitter cry :
' Rahere ! Rahere ! Ah, God ! and can it be,
My darling dead ?   Rahere ! My life ! Rahere !'

Hard by a settle stood, of oak, and black
With pass of years—rich carved of monkish craft,
With wingèd monsters ribbed and tailed, and wreaths
Most fanciful and laboured.   Lifting up,   ·
With bitter moan, her droop and yielding form,
He bore her to the seat, and laid her down,
His arm beneath her head—the lovely head
That yester-eve made pillow of his breast,
Her so desirèd haven !
                            Kneeling, he
In agony bent o'er her, oft and oft
Kissing the lips, still warm, that nevermore,
Alas ! might heed the fire of lover kiss,
Or yield him somewhat back of sympathy.

Grief-martyred nevermore, upon her face
Was peace supreme, ineffable ; no trace
Of passion conflict left, nor sorrow, loss ;
But only peace, with look of glad surprise,
As one that unexpectant greeteth friend,
Long loved, but long time parted.

So she lay,
Heav'n-tranced, and calm as chrisom babe asleep,
While o'er her wept her lover ; and the storm
Rolled on, and all the darkling fane was loud
With mortal lamentation, and the voice
Of God, in accents thunderous, that drowned
The crying of His creature, frenzy-wild.

XI.

Far otherwise than when he came the youth
Returned to Beech Hill and his dying sire.
Then rode he all impatience—eager, full
Of honest penitence for guilty wish
Scarce urged than hated. Then, in thought, he saw
The glad surprise o'erspread her angel face,
He at her feet remorseful—in his ears
The music of her weeping, on his lips
Her kisses, firstfruits of forgiveness, seals
Of fresh-pledged love, more lasting from its jar.

Now rode he sullen, careless. On his breast
His head was drooped, or lift with fevered eyes
Up to the stars, that now, the storm o'erpast,
Shone out the purple gloom, as ills of earth
Were things too small to touch them in their course
Or quench one spark of glory. In his heart
Was bitter wrath against all things, but most
'Gainst him that Godlike 'gat him, but to mar
The life he bade to being. So the lad,
The night half spent, rode homeward.

                                   Sighing deep,
He passed the lonely graveyard.   ' Ah, my sweet !
'Tis then no grand-dam fable, old wives' tale !
For thee the corpse-light burned, hell-kindled flame ;
Would now for me, accursèd spark of ill,
Thou didst like office.   Ah, Rahere ! Rahere !
Curse on ye stars ! that now so bragly shine,
My darling dead !   Could ye no influence bring,
Beneficent, to quell the gath'ring storm,
Or quench the death-winged dart that 'voiding shapes
Unclean, could only slay sweet innocence?
Out ! out ! upon the governance that gives
Loose rein to powers of evil, forces, laws,
That smite the pure and beautiful—evade
Ignoble souls and vile.

          *   *   *   *   *

                              ' How didst thou glide,
Dear love, across my life's dull firmament,
A moment gladd'ning all my way with light—
My way henceforth hedged every side with gloom,
The deeper thousandfold for glimpse of joy !
Dead ! and I live !   Ah, might I but behold
Thee once again, my darling !—clasp thee—kiss
Thy virgin lips, and clasping, kissing, die !
Ah, God, the bliss !
                              And dost thou mourn her too,'
He sighed some while thereafter, nearing home,
' Delight, good horse, thou whinniest so ?   No more—
Ah me !—her hand shall smooth thy glossy neck ;
Herself, sweet burthen, press thy willing back ;
Her voice—alas its music should be stilled !—

Fill full thine ears with gladness, as mine eyes
To overflow of tears for very thought.
Would also I were dead ! Unhappy me !
That still must live, curse-burdened evermore
With fardel of remembrance, healing Time
May never lift from off my bleeding heart !
Rahere, sweet spirit ! canst not harbinger
My soul to thine, so I be guiltless still
Of life-breach self-inflict of misery ?'

Thus he, dejected, made complaint to star,
And breeze, and tree, and shadowy shapes of night ;
Till home returned, the steward at the porch
Met him with eager speech : ' He draws to end,
And calls you often.'
                    ' Let him call !' the lad
Made answer madly.   ' All my life he shaped
Awry, and now—curse on him !—dying, leaves
Me legacy of irremissive loss !'
Amazed the old man heard : ' Nay, never curse,
Dear lad, a dying man, and he your sire !'
' Ay, sire, but never father !' swift returned
The youth with bitter irony.   ' He 'gat
Me truly, Gilbert, and thereafter naught.
I owe him nothing for the feat but hate.'

And going in thereafter—bidden oft
Of leech, and them that stood about the bed—
The lad stood angry, till his father waked
From drowse again, and one announced him nigh.
' I cannot see you, lad,' the dying man

Moaned feebly ; 'give me yet again your hand.'
But he refused.   'I'll give thee naught but hate,'
He said, while all, astonished, stopped their ears,
'For all the evil done by thee to me,
My dead love, and my mother !   Her you killed
By coldness ere her prime, too gentle soul
To habitate with such flint-hearted mate !
Not her you wedded, but her land and gold,
Which won, you dammed the current of her life
With icy barricade of chill neglect !
The better so for me, for love must forth,
And bleeding hearts bless something ere they break.
And now—and now, as this were not enough,
Your hateful lust of gold, your avarice,
Has slain the noblest, purest maid that e'er
Trod earth, to wake anew within its breast
Mem'ries of Eden !
                    Vile ! I spake the words,
Not dreaming every accent dagger stab
To her pure soul, but urged thereto alone
Of you, by you.   Great God, I, too, should weigh—
True grasper-son, dross-hearted egotist !—
In scale with thee, Rahere, a miser's spoil,
Hell-gotten hoard !'
                    Sir Edward doubtless heard
And understood, for all within his ears,
Death-touched, the surge of ebbing life made dull
And drowsing murmur.   Yet again he sighed,
And moved uneasy ; feebly lift his hand,
And prayed with spasm movement of his lips :
'Forgive me ; I am dying !'

Faint and slow
The words came forth, so full of agony
The lad could not but feel within his heart
Some echo of the woe that gave them birth.
Now part relenting, felt he once again
Beat at the portals of his stormy soul
Rahere's last blessing, sad but sweet farewell :
'God bless thee, Edward, darling ! I forgive !'

Now sprang his tears. His heart again grew soft,
As heavenly pity vanquished earthly hate,
And judgment thought gave sentence 'gainst himself :
'Thou sinnedst but to find forgiveness. Now
Canst, stern, withhold it from a dying sire ?'
'Forgive !' once more the failing man implored,
His voice but feeble whisper. O'er him now
His son bent weeping.
                    'Father, I forgive !'
He said, and from his heart ; then kissed the brow,
Death-dewed ; then took and pressed the icy hand
That hardly gave back pressure. 'I forgive !
Forgive me also, broken heart did birth
Unfilial speech ! Deliracy of grief
Alone did mouth upbraiding.'
                         Ere an hour,
Far parted, son and father each his course
New entered. This to prove what unknown spheres
Hold for the soul unfettered, what award
The spirit present meeds the mortal past ;
And this of foreset ill to fashion right,
And nobler play the man from sting of wrong

Endured, with healthful recollection stern
Of wrong projected, only not achieved
Through hinderance of virtue, not his own.

XII.

Beside the prior's tomb Rahere was laid,
For so her lover willed.   Sir Edward now,
And rich, his wish to all about was law.
A marble slab he placed upon her grave
With only this, ' Rahere,' cut deep therein.
A monument more costly far than queen's
He had upraised, but knew the pomp had jarred
Her simple soul ; so gave instead the gold
In charity to some about the fane
That dwelt in poverty, her whilom friends.

Thereafter while he brooded, taking care
For naught, his sorrow greater day by day,
Came news : the Scots, their young king at their head,
Had marched for England !
                              He was Royalist,
So why not strike a blow for Church and king ?
What matter all men said the enterprise
Was mad—the time unripe—disaster doomed,
While Cromwell, martial mystery, uplift
His sword, within whose shadow lurked defeat
Grim and resistless ?   Death !   And what to him
Was Death but kind, all-healing leech, whose hand,
Life-stilling, laid its fever memories
To sleep, like easeful opiate conqu'ring pain.

It should be so.   Concealed in secret place
The mammon labour of his father's life,
He to the West would hasten, place his sword
At service of the king for good or ill.
So bade he now old Gilbert to his room,
And, first the old man sworn to secrecy,
Laid bare his loyal purpose and his plan.

' Bide you at home,' the steward earnest urged,
His senile fear o'ercoming loyalty ;
' These scurvy Scots, who sold the martyr king,
Will never rouse our English gentry up.
No good comes out of Scotland, only plague
Of hungry lordlings.   Stay you then at home,
Sir Edward.   Noll will break them, as he brake
Duke Hamilton in Preston's three-day fight.
You cast both life and fortune to the winds,
If now you venture.   Wait, the king is young.'

Sir Edward smiled.   ' Good Gilbert, wealth to me
Is valueless, my gentle consort lost.
Death has no terror ; life no charm to keep
My sword in's scabbard.   I shall seek the king,
With just enough of gold to gild my youth
To manhood, in his royal highness' sight.
The rest I'll hide.   Nay, never think to change
My settled purpose.   I am well resolved :
What will be, will.   But yet for you, old friend,
I make a due provision.   Well I know
The Parliament will confiscate th' estate
And hall, with aught the prating knaves can find
To glut their greedy appetite for spoil.

Your faithful service here, lifelong, will count
But little with the greasy hypocrites,
Who'll flout your gray head, gibe your honesty,
And callous bid you henceforth beg or starve.
But this will balk them. I have drawn a deed
This very day, by which for service done
My father I do give thee and thy heirs
The cottage at Cock Fosters, nigh the road,
With curtilage and all appurtenance.
This open ; for the rest a thousand pounds,
To do with as thou wilt.'
                              The steward here
Had interposed ; but calmly putting by
His words, the youth continued :
                                        ' In the grot,
Beneath the water passage, we will hide
My father's ill-got gain.   'Tis well concealed
Already, and hard by ; but yet the hall
Some time may be dismantled, burnt, destroyed.
If so be that I come again, the gold
Will useful prove ; if not, then let it lie.
Or, better still, if that thou seest wrong
Adone to friend or fellow—wrong that gold
Can salve or cure—then take whate'er thou wilt ;
But, prithee, keep the secret to thyself.
My horse Delight I give to Farrier Gould,
In keeping and remembrance.'
                              Here the tears
Blinded Sir Edward's sight.   He turned aside
His face awhile to hide his manly grief.
' I am no coward, Gilbert, as thou know'st ;

So mock not thou thy master's grief, nor deem
His sword in fray will latest leap its sheath
For lover sorrow. Often hast thou praised
My mother ; oft proclaimed her paragon
Of gentleness and virtue ; said beside—
While I did love thee for such honest word—
Hadst given thy life for hers, had reaper Death
But swerved his equal sickle at thy wish ;
Such had I brought again, as fair, as sweet,
To bless all hearts and eyes with loveliness.
No more, no more of her, or I shall weep
Mine eyes so dull, some Roundhead blade will reach
My heart or e'er I shall perceive 'tis drawn.'
    *   *   *   *   *
At night, all else asleep, Sir Edward bore—
With aid of Gilbert, murmuring still regret—
Gold, jewels, deeds, in secret to the grot
That overlooked the lake. A hidden way
Ran thither from the hall, and underneath
A niche for lamp they made a privy place,
And hid the golden hoard.
                        ' Lie there, thou dross !
Whose love doth curse poor earth with larger ill
Than all hell's malice. Thou canst closer cramp
Man's soul than all the hundred ills of life ;
Canst blind his eyes ; let love engender hate
'Twixt parents, children ; mothers panders make
Of their own daughters ; good men change to churls,
Foul alchemist ! that heaven itself to hell
Would turn, once thither. Lie thou here, accurst,
Till godly use shall exorcise the ban
Of guilt upon thee !'

Thus the youth, his foot
Set on the gold, contemptuous, ere he threw
The ready earth upon it—piteous earth,
That hides so long she may the glittering dust,
Whose glamour, like to wisp-fire of the night,
Leads all her sons astray to loathsome depths
Of murk and mire.
                    ' Art sure thou hast enough,
Old friend ?   If not, take what thou wilt at will,
Nor after spare for others, be there need.'
          *   *   *   *   *
Next day Sir Edward rode again to town.
' Ah, gate ! to stand so firm, immovable,
Mocking at storm and tempest ; careless all
Who treads thy time-worn chambers, knight or cit,
And she that made thee lovely gone for aye !
Ah, lattice ! that for me shall nevermore
Unfold, to yield me glimpse of Paradise !
Away, good horse, away !   Away, Delight,
Ere thought unman me !'
                    So Sir Edward sighed,
And, quickening pace, drew up at Farrier Gould's.
Few words of greeting passed, but kindly grasp
Of hand, long held, spake much.   Then Gould, his guest
Flung careless on a settle, spake him low :
' Your bidding's done, Sir Edward.   For the child
They take your gift, and send you thanks ; but yet
Too great they deem your bounty for her state.
Cecile herself will nothing know awhile.
Sometime and hence they'll gently break the news,
And let her weep an hour upon the grave.

Grief ever comes apace, and aye too soon ;
'Tis sin to swell life's stream of bitterness
With rill of childhood tears.'
        ' Ay, let her think
So long she may, her sister lives.   Would I
Could dream such dream, nor know awakening !   Gould,
For your good service, thanks.   Now here's Delight ;
You'll keep our pact ?   No rider but yourself,
With easy task so long the brute shall live—
Your own, the worst befallen me in field !
The worst !   Ah, no, sure medicine for ill !

' Once more I'll go and look upon the stone,
The flinty cell that prisons evermore
Earth's fairest flower, heav'n-plucked, whose look of love
Burns in my soul, and aye must thrill and burn ;
Then home, and so to Oxford and the war.
Farewell, your hand ; and yet again farewell !'

PART II.

I.

WHERE Teme, in haste to join Sabrina's wave—
His sister stream—laves Broadmore's fertile field,
The Scotchmen's army waited morn and him,
Lord of all England, not by accident
Of birth, but right of royal attribute,
Pre-eminence in policy and war.

Outnumbered and out-generalled, the troops—
Their one and only argument despair—

Lay in their tents impatient, knowing well
The end had come, when Cromwell Ironside,
Swift on their track, came out the conquered North.
Repelled of all the land, hemmed in, at bay,
None thought of flight, but only of the fray,
Content to die, might each but slay his man,
And, fallen, sleep befitting warrior sleep,
Head pillowed proud on prostrate foeman's breast !

Thus lay they in the field.   Some sleeping, calm,
As Death would not at breaking of the day
Exultant stride the plain ; his lethal darts
Belch from a hundred brazen throats, whose roar
Bade the earth quake, and heav'n distressful hear ;
Would not in flash of sword or gleam of spear
Bid back to sleep of nothingness the host
But newly waked at morn from dream of home,
Wife, mother, children.
                  Others, watchful, waked,
And prayed the God of battles.   Some, again,
Made merry—careless, reckless souls, whose lands,
Whose gold, whose all, free given, had long been lost
In royal cause ; yet, loyal still, their lives,
Devotion's last and noblest gift, could now
Lay down, and smile the while their doom drew on.

These last Sir Edward Hewett comraded,
But not of choice, though never thought of prayer
Woke in his soul, morose of misery !
Through difficulties manifold, at length
The city reached where lay the royal troops,
The youth had been conducted to the king,

Who gave him courteous greeting, praising much
The loyalty that brought him to his side.
Thereafter, named for service with a troop
Of hot-blood Cavaliers, the click of dice,
And chink of gold, oft changing ownership,
With noisy oaths amany, filled his ears,
·With ribaldry that woke disgust, and oft
Drave him without the tent's lascivious fold.

To-night the mirth was purer, sense of all
The morn would bring—disaster, death, or flight
Dishonourable, did not the Lord of war,
Against all hope, work miracle—somewhat
Restraining grossness.   Nigh the entrance sat
Sir Edward, so the soft September air,
Made fragrant of the orchard's ripening fruit,
Might fresh his brow and drive away the reek
Of Spanish weed, slow-burning, and the breath
Of spirit-waters lavish poured and shared.

Now rose a clamour : 'Sing, Sir Gervase, sing !
Who knows how soon some Roundhead blade shall slit
Thy throat, and still for aye mellifluous song !
Nay, sing what wilt, man, so it be a song,
The better with a burthen, so it help
To drive away this damned despondency,
That dulls alike the edge of wit and sword !'
Then sang one, scornful miming nasal twang
Of Puritan opponent ; oft his eyes
Turned pious upward, while the rest beat time
With heel or cup, and made the canvas shake
With chorus ringing far along the field.

SONG.

Out in the fens where the cropheads abide—
   Down, Nolly, down, with thy pestilent crew !—
Satan one day in a passion outcried—
   Down, Nolly, down, with thy pestilent crew !—
'This England's so godly, but few can I damn;
I'll spawn me an imp from some lecherous dam,
So much like a saint none shall know him for sham !'
   Down, Nolly, down, with thy pestilent crew,
      Fiend-taught impostors, malignant and fell !
   Long time the land shall thy devilry rue ;
      Down, demon, down, to thy father in hell !

So Satan betook him to Huntingdon town—
   Down, Nolly, down, with thy pestilent crew !—
In garb of a leader he went up and down—
   Down, Nolly, down, with thy pestilent crew !—
A brewer's wife saw him ; ' Come in, sir, I pray ;
I need ghostly comfort ; my goodman's away.'
He went, and what came on't, there needs not to say !
   Down, Nolly, down, etc.

Thus gotten, young Nolly, 'gan erelong to bawl—
   Down, Nolly, down, with thy pestilent crew !—
Would snuggle and snuffle in cottage and hall—
   Down, Nolly, down, with thy pestilent crew !—
The whites of his eyes he'd turn up in a trice,
Did maid but anear him ; yet had she her price,
Young Nolly would pounce her like cat upon mice.
   Down, Nolly, down, etc.

So clever was Nolly, that Lord of the Fen—
Down, Nolly, down, with thy pestilent crew !—
The cuckolds now called him; how chuckled he then!—
Down, Nolly, down, with thy pestilent crew !—
Next sent him to London, he did them so brown,
Their Parliament member for Cambridge old town,
This devil-got student in trencher and gown !
 Down, Nolly, down, etc.

Who now like our Nolly, so fierce and so stout ?—
Down, Nolly, down, with thy pestilent crew !—
Our fen-dog so burly with rubicund snout—
Down, Nolly, down, with thy pestilent crew !—
At Church and at monarch he'd bark day and night,
His tongue tipped with venom, his heart full of spite,
Till he set all the city and kingdom alight !
 Down, Nolly, down, etc.

Then laid he his paw upon patten and plate—
Down, Nolly, down, with thy pestilent crew !—
Turned churches to stables, hell-cub designate—
Down, Nolly, down, with thy pestilent crew !—
Yet kept of his father from bullet and blade
In skirmish and battle, his fiend part he played
Till the martyr lay murdered, by Scots-men betrayed.
 Down, Nolly, down, etc.

Yet dies the king never ! Drink, drink to the king !—
Down, Nolly, down, with thy pestilent crew !—
The Lord's own anointed, his praises we'll sing—
Down, Nolly, down, with thy pestilent crew !—

But whisper his name, and each sword from its sheath
Leaps greedy of vengeance.   So long we have breath
We'll serve him, nor render but only to Death.
   Down, Nolly, down, with thy pestilent crew,
     Fiend-taught impostors, malignant and fell !
   Long time the land must thy devilry rue ;
     Down, demon, down, to thy father in hell !

So shouted they with often oath and threat
Of vengeance, did but Heav'n befriend the right
In coming conflict.   After, drank the health
Of wife or mistress, or court fair renowned
For beauty, grace, or winning innocence.
Then he that sang bade other sing—a lad
Of noble face, broad brow, and fearless eye
Where valour shone, with honour ingenite.
Yea, such an one as gentler times and calm
Had surely lift to height of eminence
'Mongst men pre-eminent for worth and wit ;
He now, but yet as part reluctant, sang :
     Chloe, fairest maid that e'er
     Lover moved to lover prayer,
       Yet all suit denying,
     Set within her sylvan nook,
     Weeps beside the prattler brook,
       Careless onward hieing.

     Chloe weeps for England's stain,
     Weeps the royal martyr slain,
       In his blood-shroud sleeping.
     ' Chloe, weep no more !' I cried,
     When the maid I thus espied
       By the riv'let weeping.

' Or if yet those tears must flow,
Pearl-drops worth a kingdom's woe,
    Let them fall for lover!
Death ne'er yields his spoil again ;
Chloe, pity lover pain,
    Some relief discover.'

Chloe then disdainful rose,
Lovelier still in anger shows,
    Cheeks indignant glowing.
'Sir, your king and mine doth live ;
Go where honour bids, and give
    Suit where suit is owing !

' Go ! the king doth call for aid ;
Were I man, nor feeble maid,
    I had lingered never !
Go ! and strike for king and land ;
Then perhaps may Chloe's hand
    Comrade thine for ever !'

' Chloe,' then I cried, 'I go !
Sweet, wilt not a kiss bestow,
    Lover-troth and token ?
Chloe, but and if for me
Soldier-fate and grave should be ?'
    Scarce the words were spoken,

Ere, upon my bosom cast,
Chloe weeping clasped me fast,
    Tend'rest love confessing ;
' Then I'll mourn thee night and day,
Virgin-bride of heav'n alway,
    Death life's ill redressing !'

'Well sung, Carew !   Your health, lad !   Chloe's, too !
An you but wield your blade with half the skill
You trolled your ditty—' Tush ! the song is naught,'
One peevish interjected—' finicking
From first to last.   But here's your health, Carew,
And here's a lay will better stir our phlegm :'

> But for three things Life were naught,
>   Wear'some toil and trouble,
> Fever-dream, illusion fraught,
>   Glister, glozer, bubble—
> So the sages all declare.
>   Whist, then, priest and preacher !
> Gentles, wisdom would you share,
>   Hearken comrade-teacher !
>
> Fill your tankards—fill, sirs, fill !
>   Each one, dull or witty ;
> Drink me now with heart and will,
>   Woman, wine, and ditty.
> These the three, and naught but these ;
>   Come ! who dare gainsay it ?
> Monk and priest, your prating cease ;
>   'Tis the truth—I say it !
> *Chorus.*—Up, then, up !   Drink, comrades, drink !
>   Scorned be he, nor pity
> Find, who now or e'er shall shrink
>   From woman, wine, and ditty !
>
> Woman first !   Down, down the wine !
>   Forfeit him that misses !
> She that sets her lips to mine
>   Gives for kisses—kisses !

She whose smile, like summer beam,
    Floods to untold gladness;
She whose beauty, Eden dream,
    Wakes with lover madness!
Chorus.—Up, then, up! etc.

    After woman, wine. Up, up!
    Drink the God-gift golden!
Toss the tankard, drain the cup,
    Mortals so beholden!
Drink the gift that drowneth care,
    Chaseth dull-eyed Sorrow,
Sparkling fires the soul to bear
    Nightmare Mis'ry's morrow.
Chorus.—Up, then, up! etc.

Music next, that lifteth man
    High as Zeus' portals,
Claiming there, ecstatic span,
    Kinship with immortals!
Drink the strain each rolling sphere
    Raises, blaze-surrounded—
Strain that e'en angelic ear,
    Hearing, hears astounded!
Chorus.—Up, then, up! Drink, comrades, drink!
    Scorned be he, nor pity
    Find, who now or e'er shall shrink
    From woman, wine, and ditty!

Song followed song, the while the gleamy wine,
Poured forth with unstint hand, went gaily round;
What need to spare, the Dawn, Day's henchman, near,
With moveless Fate, high-priest of callous Death,

Already waiting nigh, libation foul
Eager to pour at feet of bloody Mars !
The wine went round.　All now in turn had sung
As whim or call exacted.　All but one,
Sir Edward; he had constant made excuse,
Content to pay the forfeit noisy claimed.
But now of drink inflamed to insolence,
One rudely bade him sing, with ribald quip
Retorting, when he made again excuse.

An insult 'twas that few beside had borne,
And anger hotly flamed the mournful youth,
And all the more his grief inclined to wrath ;
But yet, his worthier impulsings obeyed,
Restraining rage, he rose and left the tent.
Then followed mocking laughter, with a word
No soldier dare forgive.
　　　　　　　　　　' No coward I,
Wine-heated fool !' he fierce rejoined, and strode
Back to the tent, and faced his challenger.
' When out thy cups I'll meet thee where thou wilt ;
But now 'twere shame to stain good honest sword
With fever-blood of sot.'　So said he, then
Smote with his glove his taunter in the face.
' So that for gage—he's friend will friend thee now,'
He added, all his anger bursting forth
And whelming prudence.
　　　　　　　　　　Blind with vinous wrath,
The Cavalier sprang up, and, drawing sword,
Made at Sir Edward.　Easily the youth
Repelled the staggering foe, and hurled him back,
Till stumbling o'er a bench he fell and lay.

Then one snatched up the glove : ' His lordship's friend
Am I, Sir Edward Hewett.   As you say,
He cannot now maintain impartial fight,
So will I for him.   Draw you, sir, and quick !'

Now drew Sir Edward back.   His anger turned
Against himself for hasty witless speech,
He had eschewed the combat ; not of fear,
But doubting much the justice of the fray.
So urged he modest : 'Sir, I spake in haste,
And pardon crave for lack of deference.
I have no quarrel save with him whose taunt
Must yet be answered and at rapier-point !
For us, the king doth need our every blade ;
Why fling away a life, nor one to spare ?'

Too deeply had they drunk to give him heed,
But rather held him fouter, coward ; bade
Him prove his challenge, or depart the tent.
So space was made, and soon the quivering steel
Sang song of conflict, strident strain that filled
The list'ners' ears with thrill of fearful joy.
The combatants were equal matched for skill,
But yet Sir Edward had advantage, since
No fever-fire of wine or vengeful rage
Flowed in his veins, or treach'rous whirled his brain.
The bright blades flashed !   How strange a thing is man !
A little while agone and on his lips
Was fierce impeachment of supernal will,
With often wish for death—life worthless all,
As so to him it seemed, his mistress dead.

14

And now for life he waged indomite fight,
Eye, hand, and brain alike at stretch to guard
The God-giv'n spark, of late so small esteemed.
Such was the thought that, flashing into mind,
E'en as he warded thrust of agile foe,
Brought scornful laugh to Edward Hewett's lip.
Enraged to fury at the fancied scorn,
The challenger pressed on.   Again the blades
Rasped vengeful ; then. from out th' assailant's hand,
The rapier flew and left him undefenced.

He, full of shame, had yet renewed the fight,
Spared of his conqueror ; but the lad Carew
With vehemence opposed : ' 'Twas fairly fought
And fairly won.   Sir Edward Hewett comes
Across all England through a world of foes
To serve the king !   But sorry welcome this,
And scurvy guerdon for his loyalty !
Shame on us all, I say !   Who next shall draw
On him, draws on me also—George Carew.'

The brawl had doubtless spread ; too young the lad
To influence older, wilder, ruder men,
Had not a shot now boomed along the plain
From out the sheltering Severn's mist-clad hills,
With answer soon from Teme's contiguous shore.
So ceased the clamour, lesser strife forgot
In imminence of conflict vast, whose throes
Should shake all England, and its issue bind.
'There goes old Noll's reveil—Fleetwood's reply,'
One said low-toned.   ' Enough of fighting now
We'll have erelong.   The Cropheads wake them soon,

As battle were but pastime, and the day
Too short for 'joyment. 'Sdeath ! they're all astir.'

The tents forsook, in groups about the field,
Already touched of Dawn's gray-shafted beams,
The soldiery gathered. 'Gainst a wattle wall
Sir Edward leaned apart from all, as so
He deemed, his thoughts afar from camp and field.
' My love ! my own ! the end is nigh !' he sighed.
' Rahere, dear heart, where'er thou dwellest now,
Make lodgment for thy lover. Life is death
Without thee, darling—death but only life !
Break, Dawn, apace ! ye shapeful mists, away !
So hopeless we may yet our fate descry,
And die, death grappling.'
                                    So he murmured low.
Then came a voice, but gently : ' Sir, forgive,
If that I come unwelcome and disturb
Heart-easing thought.' Sir Edward hasty turned.
The lad that late had championed his cause
Stood graceful by him. He for sole reply
Stretched out his own and grasped the other's hand,
But after spake him warmly :
                                    ' I am much
Your debtor, and for courtesy forgot
Of all our comrades.'
                                    ' Ay, we did you wrong,'
The boy replied, light laughing. ' True the saw,
" When wine is in, then wit is ever out."
You bare yourself full nobly. I did ill
To speak so late, and pardon crave therefor.

What think you of our hap ; is't desperate,
As most do say, or have you comelier hope ?'

Sir Edward smiled.   ' I have no hope but this,
Our comrades, so courageous facing friend,
Will prove so valorous towards sturdy foe
That naught shall stand before them.   For the rest,
The country all about us is in arms.
But that I saw it, wondering, for myself,
I had not thought, nor aye believed, the land
So firm resolved to stand against the king.
How 'tis were hard to fathom ; but the heart
Of England beats to-day for Parliament,
And Parliament in Cromwell.   This the speech
I heard in hostel, where I lay the night
Before I reached the city :
                              " King of Scots,"
One said in scorn, "and crowned in Edinbro' !
Chief Judas then, arch-traitor to the dead !
So let him reign in Scotland an he may !"

' So all agreed, while yet another cried :
" Beside, 'tis said he signed the Covenant ;
How must his sire have turned him in his grave !
I lift no hand for renegade, to bring
Scotch locusts like a murrain on the land."
Then hummed they all applause.
                              ' No hope !   The land,
Part dazzled by the star of victory,
That baleful sits on Cromwell's rugged brow,
Part stilled by weariness of strife, dislike
Of aught that's Scottish, lies supine or moves

Complacent thrall to pike-hedged Parliament.
What boots, then, this our force of aliens, set
Against a kingdom martial and in arms?
I know the thought thou wilt reject with scorn,
Nor hold him friend whose lips shall counsel flight;
But yet, Sir George, if thou wouldst see again
Thy Chloe——'
        Here the lad impatient hand
Laid on the speaker's arm. 'How know you that
I sang of self? Your other speech is naught,
Else had Sir Edward Hewett never come
Through ever-present danger to his king.'

'Thy soul was in the song,' the knight replied,
'And, as I think, did pen it. Lover ears
Are sharper than of common. I am here,
In truth, the more for love of buried maid
Than sake of king unproved, untried, or fate
Of country, self-subdued, content to lie
Gyved at the foot of rustic conqueror.'

'Why, so with me,' Sir George returned. 'Alas!
Our house is much divided; some for king,
Some Parliament. Till Edith spake me so,
I troubled not for either. Since we stand
Thus equal moved and circumstanced, let's make
True compact. He that 'scapes the battle doom
Shall bear fond message to his comrade's fair.'
Sir Edward laughed. 'Small hope of that, but yet
I promise. Give me then your lady's name.'
This did the lad with token, and a word
Or two of love, rough pencilled in the dawn,

And sealed with tears not unobserved by him
That took and laid the trifle safely by.
' Now you, Sir Edward.'
　　　　　　　Then he solemnly :
' Thy sins, Sir George, can be but few ; too young
And fresh thy soul from Maker's hand for sin
To soil and mar to utter jeopardy,
So Death to thee may be but claviger
To Paradise.　If I, less fortunate,
Should fail to-day to know Life's turmoil done,
But, earth-curst, still must linger—like to him
The undying wretch that day by day must drag
His penance-weighted being up and down　, .
Unsympathetic earth, Death longing, while
Ever the farther Death doth fly for prayer—
Then thou, so soon amid ecstatic throng
Thou seest one beyond conception fair,
Where all are beautiful, then wilt thou know
My soul's earth-ravished saint, heav'n-stol'n Rahere !
Then tell her this : her lover's heart did break
Of penitence what time impatient heav'n
Her short-lent prodigy bid back again—
Too pure, too fair, the maid for aught but clasp
Of kindred spirits, stainless, passionless !
Tell her a thousand kisses I did set
Upon her lips, death-cold, that yet no chill
Gave to my frenzied soul's self-torturing fire.
Say how, with myriad blistering tears, her shroud—
The snow-white bride-gown of her peerless form—
I dewed, till careful grand-dames cried me shame !
Ah me ! the cold, cold hand that lay in mine,

All careless of caressing ! God ! the smile
Sweet lingering on her lips, but not for me !
Her wondrous look——'
                    Abruptly ceased the knight,
Strode forth a little way, then quick rejoined
His wondering comrade.   Spake him slow again :
' Sir George, my heart is charnelled with the dead—
Life evermore a burden !   Judge you, then,
How small the chance I prove Love's messenger
To any but my own lost paragon !
Best seek another likelier far to live.'

Then answer made the lad with sparkling eye :
' Nay, nay ; I leave the matter where it is.
No messenger for Love like sorrowing love.
A hundred times I'll chance the rather you,
Than any of our comrades, telling tale
Of loss, with hunger-wakened eyes the while
Feasting on beauty doubly beautiful
For added charm of cheek-impearling tear.
But yet for me, forgive me, artless foe
To Time's all-healing leechcraft, I did probe
A wound so deep and cruel as your own
To throb and throe of fresh-awakened pain.'

II.

Now brake the day of doom !   Yet sometime hung
The brooding mist o'er all the fateful plain,
Distressful Nature loath to lift the screen
That yet a little while her matron breast
Benignant kept from stain of offspring blood.

Now waxed the sun impatient, careless he
Whate'er Earth's children of their pigmy pride
Wrought to their hindrance, so his healthful beam,
Escaped anew the gloom of night-throned deep,
Diffused its softening gladness every side.
Anon the wind, peace-wearied, here and there
Smote at the vap'rous canopy, that now,
Slow-moving, 'gan dispart, when swift the sun
His golden sheen drove wedgeway all between
The tearful, trembling cloud till all was gone.

Meanwhile the foe, beneath the friendly haze
Concealed, his task pursued without annoy ;
And now, his floating causey consummate,
O'er Teme and Severn poured his stern array.
Silent they came, as scornful of the Scot,
Nor needing cheer of comrade shout, nor aught
Of 'couragement beyond the warrior fire
That burned in each, with confidence in him
Who led them, first to print the hither shore
With hostile foot contemptuous.
                              On they came,
A mighty host resistless as the sea
That, man's frail rampire stormed, fierce chafing leaps
With arched and spumy mane upon the land.

Nor lay the Scotsmen still.   Himself secure
From all the fateful chances of the fray,
The Stuart, off the minster tow'r, beheld
His foes advance, led of his chiefest foe,
And gave command to check their onward way.

Now angry spake the iron mouths of war,
With thunderous roar that rent their canopy
Of wreathing smoke illumed of leaping flame ;
Yet came they on—he at their head, who scorned
Less danger than the least of all the host
His willing war-mates.   Onward came they still,
For all the hurtling hail, unmoved, unchecked ;
Not silent now, for out a thousand throats,
Drowning war's discord and the deafening tramp
Of marching myriads, rang the battle-cry,
' The Lord of Hosts !' as when the Dunbar hills
Shrank at the shout, far borne along the main,
That, startled, stilled his billowy turbulence,
Amazed at tumult vaster than his own.

Now led by troop of dare-all Cavaliers,
The Scotsmen boldly braved the iron flood
Of pike and sword and gaping arquebus.
'Twas all in vain ; the steely tide swept on,
For all the conflict shock of 'countering wave.
In vain, now here, now there, despairing might
A little while would stem the fell advance,
The battle surge rolled, noisy, ever on,
O'er bleeding wrecks of manhood, gasping sore
For life beneath the trampling foot of friend
Or foe alike unheedful.
                              On they came,
With ever at their head him, Ironside,
His sad, keen eyes observant every way
Of each and all—of him that doughty bore
Himself as hero, or that blenched the fight.

Composed and calm, yet ne'er impassive, rode
Awakened England's chief of men ; full oft
A word of cheer upon his lips for them
That needed—ofter, praise for warrior deed
Well done—with ever in reserve the flame
Of scathing anger, swift as summer flash,
Did any thwart, neglect, or disobey.

A hillock, sharp contested, now was won,
And now the Scots, disheartened, gave amain.
Upon the knoll-top Cromwell, halting, saw
Where, in the broken fight, two Cavaliers
Fought fiercely, so a rally might be made.
Then lit his steely eyes with kindred fire :
' Who are the lads?' he asked of him that rode
Beside him, post at need and adjutant.
' The nearer is but boy, dame's parlour yet
Befitting more his years than battle-field !
They should be brothers—see, the elder guards
The younger ! Ha, well warded ! Saw you that ?
Go, give the striplings quarter ! Pity 'twere
To nip such manhood promise in the bud !'
But now, fresh rallied, stood the Scots again.
Again the turmoil heightened, and the fate
Of these forgotten in the larger need,
Cromwell anew moved on unconquerable.
Yet fought they stubborn till the word ran round,
' Retire ! retire ! all's o'er at Powick Bridge !'
Retire ! or else they take us in the rear !'
So did they, sorely harassed in retreat,
And saved alone from rout by friendly hedge,

And wooded lane, and orchard garth that brake
The ranks of charging horsemen, and forbade
Destruction to the death of gallant foe.

Meanwhile the Teme at Powick larger ran,
Fed, ghastly, from a thousand rills of life !
Strown with the dead, like wrack on storm-beat shore,
His trampled banks lay horrid.   All the noon
Keith and Montgomery here with Fleetwood strove,
Until his chief, his strategy complete,
Threw troops o'er Teme to help his warlike son ;
Then, beaten, fled they, till the city walls
Received them, and its flinty barrier set
Awhile betwixt the victor and his prey.

    *   *   *   *   *

'Twas hour for prayer, yet few within the fane
Were gathered..   These the boom of nearing war
Heard in their ears, with blare of trumpet-call
And tramp of hurrying squadrons.   Past the pile
Fair Severn seaward lapped her gelid stream,
Fresh from the Cymry hills, all careless she,
So long her mountain tribute she might bear
To ocean undisturbed, whate'er befell
The frenzied host that thronged her fertile shores.

Within went trembling up the prayer for peace,
And light in darkness ; then, above the din—
Each moment more tumultuous—little while
Rose mighty harmonies, that, rolling, filled
The fane magnifical, befitting Him
Of whom, to whom, the glorious descant rang :

The Lord descended from above,
 And bowed the heavens most high,
And underneath His feet He cast
 The darkness of the sky.
On cherubs and on cherubim,
 Full royally He rode,
And on the wings of mighty winds
 Came flying all abroad.

So soared the anthem up. Then followed prayer
For him, shamed England's after-bane, who now
Stood at the minster threshold, bidding back
His beaten host to shelter of the walls
Of loyal Worcester, faithful to her fall !

There sheltered safe, they courage took of shame
And anger at defeat, and loudly cheered
A sally planned against the victor's camp,
His forces still the most part o'er the stream.
Now woke again the Severn hills in wrath,
Man's thunder dull re-echoing far and near.
Fierce charged, the Roundheads' threefold ring of steel
Erelong gave way. Sometime disorder reigned,
While hope 'gan flicker in the Stuart breast.
Fell was the fight and bloody. Neither side
Or pity showed or sought ; each combatant,
His soul aflame with rage and battle-lust,
Fought as of old his berserk fathers fought,
Nor knew of wound or hurt till stealing Death
Tugged sudden at his heartstrings and he fell.
'Twas push of pike 'gainst pike, 'twas sword to sword,
With ever in their clang'rous greeting, death ;

Or flash of petronel in face of foe,
Whom Death alone bade bar no more the way.
Thus for a time did traitorous Fortune smile
On sturdy Scot and charging Cavalier.
Back driven, the Roundheads scowling fell, no man
But with his face toward his enemy.
Yet still they gave, outnumbered—trodden down
By squadrons charging like to hurricane,
Hill born, that furious cleaves its havoc way
Through shrieking woodlands swept from out its path !

'Again, brave hearts ! again, and all is won !'
So cried the royal leader, and a shout
Went up and bade the wood-topt hills resound
Untimely note of triumph. On they dashed
Impetuous, fearless, noble souls that waged
Ignoble war, for princely churl, against
Their truer nature and their country's weal.

But hark, o'er all the thunder of their charge,
The shout of new-come warriors, horse and foot !
See him at head whose star did never pale
In fight, whose presence gives a hundred heart
To shock a thousand. As at morn, the word
Breaks from his lips, ' The Lord of Hosts !' and all
His thousands shout it, till the mighty roar
Knocks at the clouds and bids the welkin hear.

Now, royal Stuart, hurl thy gallant might
'Gainst his, the might of God-giv'n majesty !
Hurl ! hurl ! to break like ocean tempest-flung
'Gainst earth, rock-guarded ! Hurl ! and shivering turn
To wuthering spray, wind-whipt, wind-tost, and spurned !

They come ! they dash ! they fall like avalanche !
As thunder loud the crash, the shock, the shout !
Death grappling now, they strike, they thrust, or e'en,
Too close for armèd conflict, clutch at throat,
Or wrist, or belt, with tiger hand and fell !
So thus awhile, till slow at trumpet-call
The charging mass recoils a breathing space ;
Then on again to meet severer fate :
For charged in turn by Ironside veterans,
They break, they flee to shelter of their foot,
Half of their strength death-garnered on the plain.

With these Carew ! Escaped the morning fray,
All day the lads had battled side by side ;
Had seen, themselves no niggards in the fight,
The royal forces thrust from post to post,
At Powick and St. Johns, till Fleetwood stood
With Lambert, waiting only courier word
From Cromwell to assault the doomèd town.

Together still the last and fatal charge
They made undaunted.   Foremost they of all
The gallant troop of English chivalry
That fearless dashed against the gates of Death,
To show the slower Scotsmen how to die.
So fierce his charge, Sir Edward clave his way
Through pike and carbine.   Still with him the boy
Some bravely followed.   Death on every side
They gave and took.   But few were left when loud
The trumpet clang its coward-toned recall.
Then fury swelled Sir Edward's soul beyond
The warrior lust of slaughter and of blood.

'I go not back!' he hissed through clenchèd teeth;
But all had turned obedient to the clang
Save the brave boy beside him.   Seeing him,
More generous thought arose : ' My life is mine
To do with as I will; but this brave lad ?'
Then turned he, too ; but as he turned, the boy
Gave sigh and fell across him.   Through his heart
A ball had ploughed from musketeer anigh,
His caliver still smoking.
                              Nothing more
Sir Edward knew, for maddening rage that numbed
His brain and stole away intelligence.
But this he did : about the dying boy
He flung his arm and snatched him to himself;
Then, vengeful, smote to death the musketeer ;
And after furious spurred his snorting horse
Against the circling, threatening ring of steel.
Thence cleaving path he gained anew the plain,
And so again the rallying troop, unhurt,
By soldier courtesy of one whose heart
Swelled at the deed, and generous forbade
His troop to fire upon him as he rode.

So rode they back together—life and death :
Life as his wont, sore burdenèd with weight
Of Death, his twin-born terror; sleepless Death
That yet doth ever boon of wakeless sleep
Bear for his comrade, grief-environed Life !

Dead was the lad!   Too soon his course at end,
The generous boy that nevermore might lie
Clasped in his Chloe's proud and grateful arms !

Weep for him, maidens !—him that maiden face,
Tear-framed and sad of still reproach, could lure
From love, to carnage, sacrifice, and death !
Weep for him, Chloe ! yet no tear shall wake
Nor sigh disturb him where he peaceful sleeps,
Lulled by the minster's soft and tuneful chime.

Beneath a tree his comrade laid him down,
And, madness past, leaned sadly o'er the boy :
'So thou art sped, dear lad, and I still live,
To whom life is but burden !   Twice to-day
Thy life I kept 'gainst him that mocking flies
Unhappy me, though sought for eagerly.

Now clang again the trumpet.   At the call,
Sir Edward, kneeling, kissed the pallid brow :
'I go in hope to follow where thou'rt gone ;
If not, then bear my message to my love,
As I to thine unwilling.'
                                    Mounting quick,
He joined the shouting troop, and once again
Dashed at the foe, slow moving o'er the plain.
Vain all ! for scarce at impact with the pikes
Were they when Cromwell charged them in his turn
On either flank, and brake them hopelessly.

          *   *   *   *   *

Slow sank the sun in cloud of blood, as heav'n
Were wrathful, and her crimson antient set
For signal, high above the heads of them
That sought again to rivet royal chains
On them by her advanced to liberty.

Then drew the evening shades about the field,
Yet still they fought, for stiffer fight was ne'er
Throughout the war, nor longer in suspense.

Of all the troop Sir Edward comraded,
But one was left. 'Twas he that, drunken, drew
Upon the youth, and for his pains was thrown.
He, sullen all the day, had kept aloof,
Distressed to know himself in bravery
So far behind the lad he late defamed.
Now Fortune willed they met, a lull in fight
Succeeding cruel onslaught. Coldly smiled
The knight, and, moved to keener speech than wont,
Made gibing challenge : ' Sir, but yester-eve
You bade me draw, of insolence alone ;
To-night I counter challenge. Yonder rides
Old Noll, as we do call him, hazarding
His life as he were meanest of them all—
A gallant charge, and haply all the war
Were ended ; all doth hang upon his life.
I do attaint you, sir, of cowardice
Unless you instant follow where I lead !'

Then he, regretful : ' I have seen this day
Sir Edward Hewett do such gallant deed
That in my soul I feel myself abased,
And freely do withdraw untruthful taunt,
With crave of pardon. Granted that, I ride
Most gladly where you will. Would that we two
Might end our country's peril with our lives,
So that our deadly errand were complete !'

15

'In wine all men are fools !'   The proverb old
The knight remembering, felt resentment go.
' Contented I ! yet follow not my lead,
If any, prayerful, watch thy coming home.
But see, it is himself that hither comes
With but a few—rides up and down.—What's that ?
Will give us quarter, lay we down our arms !
'Twere best we did, for hark how Fleetwood storms
At Worcester gates !   Ay, best indeed for these
Poor Scottish sheep, led forth to butchery !
So—shot for answer !   Rugged courtesy
For proffered mercy, that !   Then 'tis the end ;
Old Noll doth ever summon thus ere falls
His doom-stroke on a brave antagonist.
There goes he back contemned !   Before again
He comes like thunderbolt, the thing I dream
Must aye be done, or left undone for aye.'

His eyes to heav'n the knight a moment lift,
Then gazed around him sternly o'er the field.
A moment marking where the dead boy lay,
His stern gaze softened ; yet did never prayer
Birth in his soul, but only, on his lips
His mistress' name soft trembled !   Then he cheered
His failing horse, and singly charged the foe.

Amazed in part, part doubtful of his end,
The nearer foe that saw his swift approach
Withheld their fire, nor harmed him as he rode
Where Cromwell, halting, spake his force in face.
But soon his errand known, upon his lips

Defiant challenge of their mighty chief,
A hundred sprang them forward, and a shout
Of warning thrilled the ranks from end to end.'

Then Cromwell turned, the danger saw unmoved—
Unmoved heard challenge—saw uplifted sword—
Smiled grimly when, death-furrowed by a pike,
The shrieking steed that bore his challenger
Fell prone, and flung his rider at his feet.
' Nay, slay him not !' he thundered forth in tone—
None dared to disobey, a hundred hands
Uplift to smite the daring enemy—
' Secure him ; I will speak the lad anon !'

So did they, some reluctant, scowling hate ;
Some nobler, letting admiration speak
In look and usage.   Cromwell nothing more
Deigned to his pris'ner, but, the end at hand,
Stormed at the Scot till all the sorrowing field
Beneath the shock of battling squadrons shook ;
Its sward, with life-ooze battening, and its brook
Bridged, loathsome, o'er with bridge of dying men,
Unholy causeway, bleeding, quivering, torn
Alike by tramp of friend and enemy,
And iron heel of charger, callous urged
To onward task of slaughter !
                    Faded out
The crimson ensign of dejected day !
Night fell, but still within the city walls
The strife went on, the shades funereal
Fringed oft and o'er with fiery sheen, and shook
With hurtling roar that woke the firmament,

To mark how man could mime ethereal war
And curse the earth with ills a thousandfold
More fell than fiend against him e'er conceived.

III.

Calm after storm ! Th' ensanguined wave of war,
Its lethal fury past, made pact with peace.
Dumb was the royal town, in grasp of hate
Victorious and leaden-tongued despair.
Melodious no more with service praise
The pillared minster rang, but mournful stood
Song-stilled, and voiceful only with the groan
Of prisoner death-wounded, or the sigh
Of them more wretched still, awaiting doom
Of slavery in stern Bostonian shore !

From hour to hour the number grew of these,
Unwilling worshippers, though often Death—
His gelid finger laid on suff'rer brow—
Spake voiceless, yet resistless : ' Friend, give place
To other ; thou art bidden upper seat !
Unearthed from cave and cellar—vain asile—
The beaten foe was haled, until no more
Of pris'ner congregation could the fane,
But stood averseful gaol, its hoary walls
And portals closely sentinelled and kept
On every side by stern-faced guards, who saw
In victory but crowning mercy, wrought
For them, by them unworthy instruments
Of Him that faithful kept His Israel,
And slumbered not nor slept.

Within the aisle,
Anigh the choir, Sir Edward Hewett stood
Beside a hundred sullen Highlandmen,
Whose looks, whose speech, though little understood,
Yet spake resentment, anger, and mislike,
That but a spark had flamed to active hate.
For was he not a Saxon, Scotia's bane?
And were they not by such as he undone?
Led from the land they loved to hopeless field
Of death, or yet more hopeless servitude?

Slow dragged the painful hours.   At noon the guard
That stood without forced back the portal door.
Then came a file of carbineers and bound
The knight all unresistful save for speech :
'What need to bind a willing captive, friends?
May I not die as knight and gentleman?'
'Be that as may,' made answer one, 'but first
Must wait the general's pleasure!   Bear him on !'

A little way they led him, then made halt
Before a gateway sentinelled, but passed
Within, the challenge given and the sign ;
Then up a cumbrous stair to sturdy door,
That smitten gave back answer faintly heard
Through heart of oak : ' Within !'   So entered they,
Saluting him that writing sat, nor looked
From off his scroll till all his task was done.

A panelled room, low-ceiled, with window broad
That gave upon the courtyard's cobbled pave—
An oval table strewn with documents,
And him thereat freed England's arbiter,

Wise helmsman of her dest'ny, cynosure
Of Europe, all astonished and afraid—
This saw Sir Edward while the victor wrote,
But not as ready writer, one to whom
The pen was facile, but with knitted brow
And often interjection, till at last,
His laboured despatch o'er, he flung aside
His style like wearied schoolboy.

      ' Ah, the lad !'
He said to him that officered the troop—
' But bound ! I bade not that. Nay, nay, too brave
The boy to turn assassin ! Set him free !
And wait without ; I may have other need.'

They gone, his mournful eyes upon the knight
The conq'ror long time set; then slowly spake :
' Come nearer, lad. Your name? Yet sit you down
In window-seat ; your weariness doth show
Full plain, for all your mask of unconcern
Again, your name ?

     Hewett, and son of him
That gave good aid in gold from time to time
When most our business needed !—Lad, what fit
Of madness drew you here, malignant, when
The Lord did purpose final overthrow
Of Belial seed, with mercy for His saints
Complete and overwhelming? Nor enough
Yourself to brave your country, but must bring
Your brother and a chit to battle doom.'

This gainsaid he. Then clouded Cromwell's brow :
' How dost Thou blind them, Lord, they cannot see,

And yet so plain to zealous eye Thy law !
Sir George Carew ! and John Carew did set
His hand with me to that which startling rang
The knell of tyranny in England ; shook
Each despot throne in Europe ; quaked each heart
That sat thereon, self-judged, with coward fear
Of righteous retribution.'
                       Silent now
The victor stood, his mighty face ablaze
With fire of indignation.   Soon again
His searching eyes surveyed the weary youth,
And milder grew at sight of pain restrained,
Yet evident in attitude and mien :
' Art hungry, lad ?   Needs must.   See, here is food,
Mine own untasted.   Mercies such as this,
Exceeding thought, do satisfy the soul—
Yea, e'en the flesh—beyond all meat and drink.'

A little ate the youth of gratitude ;
Then stayed again the warrior in his walk,
And spake him not unkindly : ' Lad, yestreen,
Where hottest showed the scrabble, marked I you,
Foe such as foe assured of victory
Might spare, and sparing honour most himself,
But friend-changed, grapple to his soul as fast
As Jonathan did David.   Boy, again
I ask what moved you glut your stripling sword
With patriot blood ?'
                   Now spake Sir Edward slow,
And otherwise than as he first designed,
His ruder thought o'erborne by courtesy

And soldier treatment : 'Sir, you claim the right
To fight for Parliament ! So I for king,
The older and, as some do deem it still,
The better cause.'
           The steely eyes flashed fire ;
The warrior's face grew stern with cold contempt
As made he ready answer : ' Boy, you speak
As one to whom fair landskip were but patch
Of painter pigments idly mingled—one
That devil-blinded argues blaze of day
But blur of sagging mist. Boy, boy ! we fought
For liberty against a trait'rous king ;
But you, of childish pity crazed, to bind—
Fresh forged of shame and vengeful enmity—
The gyves we brake so late from off your limbs.
Hast never heard of Leighton ? Elliot pined,
Brave honest heart, to death in royal gaol ?
Monopolies and fines ? Star Chamber law,
Against all mercy, justice, evidence?
Decrees against all freedom ? Penalty
Of cell and stripes for them that dared assert
A royal proclamation never law ?
Truth manacled of prelacy, with faith
And conscience buffeted of hireling priests ?
These were the ills that drave us after long
And patient parley to th' arbitrament,
The sharp but wholesome judgment of the sword.
I tell thee, lad, had we not fall'n to arms
Against Charles Stuart and his tyrannies,
Our children and their children's children shame
Had cried upon our manhood !

That we did
His will therein, who setteth up the meek,
And hurleth oft the tyrant out his seat,
Is plain in this, that ever on our side
The God of battles fought, until we beat
Our haughty foes as small as garner dust,
And trod both king and prelate hopeless down !'

Thus Cromwell, ever more and more his voice
Thrilling with rugged eloquence, until
The chamber vocal rang as clarion call
Voiced wall and panel.   Silence following on,
Strange sense Sir Edward felt of littleness,
As one in unthought presence of a soul
A world above his own.   Some little while
In silence either gazed upon his foe,
Then Cromwell spake again: 'Thou'rt but a boy,
And I a fool to take thee at thy word;
Yet, lad, I like thy spirit, and would prove,
Late foe, new friend. 'Twas but a brainless freak
That brought thee hither; all the land beside
Unmoved, or only moved to disavow
Part in the madman project of the Scot,
And him their two-faced puppet, called their king !
Change sides.   Henceforth the steely arbiter
Untroubled dwells in's sheath, yet earnest souls
May find enow of conflict e'en in peace
To sate the battle instinct of the man.
The war is o'er; 'twas hopeless from the first
For them that took the trap I crafty set :
Not but '—and here the rugged face lit up

With soldier admiration—'thousand such
As thee had natheless given me larger task.
But yet a word : what project hadst thou, lad,
So madly charging down, and all alone ?
'Tis thought to take me unaware——'

                                          ' No, no !'
The knight brake forth while Cromwell keenly heard ;
' Not that ! I am no murd'rer. All was lost
Did not some happy chance retrieve the day.
'Twas life for life : I called thee as I came—
Had never struck thee wardless.'

                                     ' So I deemed,'
The victor answered, smiling. ' More, methought
I heard thee challenge, but some said me nay.
Good lad, 'twas folly. He doth hedge about
His saints so sure they get them never harm.
A thousand fall beside them, yet they stand ;
Nor night nor day know terror, but repose
Beneath His wings safe-bucklered and assured.'

Thus Cromwell, fervent, while Sir Edward sighed :
' In truth 'twas folly, but for hope of that
All day so vainly sought, and aye denied,
Death, that doth end with greatly-welcome dart
Loss and remorse, with pang of viper shame.
Yet am I glad my enterprise did fail ;
'Twas battle frenzy leagued with inscient thought
Of thee, far other than persuades me now.
Be that enough of that. But, for the rest,
Whate'er befall I cannot do your will,
My loyalty fast pledged to saintly dead.'

Then Cromwell spake again with knitted brow :
' Past comprehension art thou, lad !   Why rush
So madly still to ruin, battle heat
No longer pleading soldier lenity?
Thy words convey a meaning far apart
From youth and boyhood's golden-footed crew.
What sorrow's thine, so deep thou biddest death
Relieve thee, and of what but common ill?
Shame on thee, lad ! despaired at first reverse
Sustained of fate, life's threshold barely crossed.
Thy father dead, thou hast a fair estate,
Or hadst, should Parliament take cognizance
Of this thy freak.   Believe me, boy, there's naught
Like wholesome toil to lift the troubled soul
Out quagmires of despair.   Take service, then,
With me, I say ; I'll bear thee safely through
The outcome of thy folly.   Know, of all
The hundreds cooped in yonder popish pile,
Few shall return to Scotland with the tale
How England mowed th' incursive thistle down.
Thus shall it ring the louder in all ears,
And longer.   Monk besides shall press it home
At sword's point, need be !'
                                    Cromwell thus, full stern,
With gleam of anger kindling in his eye
Whene'er he named the Scotsmen.   Slowly now
Sir Edward made rejoinder :
                                    ' From my heart
I thank you for your proffer, but will share
Plantation or the gibbet with the rest,
Or e'er I break the pledge I gave the dead.

PART III.

I.

SLOW roll the years, a weary tale to him
Fore-doomed to bear the burden of remorse,
Life's weightiest fardel, bound to wand'rer back !
Love's hunger joined to constant sense of loss
And Tantal dream of all that might have been
But for some deadly self-inflicted shock,
What need to feign the fallacy of hell,
The soul its own Gehenna?
                              Harassed thus,
Sir Edward Hewett ever restless moved,
His sword at call of any save the Turk ;
Careless whate'er the enterprise, so long
It crost not soldier's honour, nor might lack
The zest of Danger, pursuivant of Death.
Self-held and silent, taking never part
In aught beside his duties—song and cup
And dice put by as things too small for scorn—
The rather had his fellows held him foe
Than friend, had not his scanty purse been first
To ope at comrade's need ; his doughty sword
Been chief in conflict ; ward, or thrust or stroke
Not seldom yielding over-fraughted mate
A timely succour !
                    Vainly courting Death,
Death fled him ever, like to woman-maid
That, wistful, yet doth shun entreative swain,
Her girl-fears conqu'ring still conservant fire !
Thus he pursuing, Death, his suppliant face

Beholding, coldly turned him otherwhere,
To slay where slaughter best his mood malign
Might fill with hope of after-bitterness !

Yet gained Sir Edward fame, and in its track
Command and wealth had followed ; but no ear
He lent ambition, while the thought of gold—
The thrice-curst source of all his misery—
His soul abhorred.   Disdainful thus, his name
Was often on fair lips, and yet the more,
However fair, no maid could win a smile
Or look, or word 'yond soldier courtesy !

So passed the years !   His frame with warrior toil
Was knit to ampler manhood.   In his port
Was dignity with consciousness of power.
His lofty brow, sunburned, was nothing marred
By canker care, which only in his eyes
Deep-dwelled, and spake of sorrow 'yond compare.

Yet had he friends ; nay more, companions—they,
That ofttimes wiser read the face of men,
As later come from heaven's all-sentient shore
Than they that bare them—eager sought him out
To share his walk or play about his path,
Glad of his stalwart manhood, and the smile—
The rare sweet smile—he kept for them alone.
These sometimes bringing gifts of flowers, one eve
A maid scarce taller than his knee held forth
A sprig of woodbine.
                    Sudden to his breast
He snatched the laughing youngling, bending o'er
The curly head to hide the surging woe

That marred his sight.   She, looking up, beheld
His sorrow, and was, child-like, moved to tears
Of angel sympathy.   So, setting down the maid,
He, in a moment master of himself,
Assuaged her grief with kiss and pleasantry :
' Nay, Blümchen, never weep !   The sun did shine
So gloriously, methought your golden head
Was all ablaze !'   So said he, and put by
The child's entreaty.
                          But at night he drew
From out his vest a silken fold that held
A sprig of woodbine, sere and crisp, the same
Rahere of old had giv'n him when he first
Revealed his love and sought responsive pledge.
This pressèd he to his lips the while his head
Lay in his hands upon the chamber board,
Till Night, Morn-challenged, yielded place to Day.

    *   *   *   *   *

It was the time that, Cromwell dead, the land—
Perplexed and torn this way and that—at length
Made terms with him upon whose head a price
Before had been determined.   With the morn
Came tidings through a comrade that the king
' His own enjoyed again,' had been received
In England as some mighty conqueror
Returned victorious after deadly grip
With foe that perilled empire.
                          ' Now for home,
And recompense for all our exile toil !
The canting knave that got old Templeton,
And for a song, when Worcester wrecked us both,

Shall quick disgorge—at sword's point an there's need. ·
When say you that we start ?   'Tis heavenly news !'

Thus he that brought the tidings.   All unmoved,
Or moved but little by th' intelligence,
The knight began : ' I go not back !   For me——'
When quick his comrade made remonstrance keen :
' Not back ! not back ! why, man, but this is worse
Than very spring-tide madness !   Not go back,
But let some cuckoo Crophead keep you out
Your proper nest !   Why, you were counted rich
Beyond us all !'
                        ' And am so still, good friend,'
The knight replied.   ' I game not, neither sink
The Godlike in the beast, nor blunt the sting
Of recollection in oblivious cup,
And so am rich beyond all wish and need.
Is't not enough ? what would your lordship more ?'
' What more, what more ! why, surely everything !
Dost never quicken pulse at maiden clasp ?
Or feel thy soul at music of a sigh
Thrill so thou heard'st celestial symphony ?
Ne'er leaps thy heart what time the clicker dice
Bring fortune——'
                        ' Ay, and thrice-felt beggary—
Remembrance ever wielding scorpion lash—
To him that cursing loses,' interposed
Sir Edward grimly.   But the other laughed :
' Sir Puritan, why, therein's half the charm—
The risk, the catch-breath expectation, flush
Of fever-blood !   But surely you will home ?'

16

'Not I !   The land has never home for me,
With none to bid me welcome of my kin ;
But only mem'ries bitter as a draught
Of grand-dam garlic.   Here at least, methinks,
Some few would miss me of the poorer sort,
And some few children.   All the world is home
To him whose thoughts are bonded nevermore
With things of earth, but heav'n.'
                              ' Ay, ay ! but, then,
'Tis time to service heav'n when earth's at end.
The country needeth men—you are of them ;
I say it not in flattery, grant me that—
Who ever must be helmsmen in a state.
The king will need good counsellors, as ships
Need ballast, and the more his hither course
Has not been of the fairest.   You may be
Whate'er you will !   When Dunkirk fell, he heard
Your part therein, and spake of Worcester field ;
And swore, long since he had been England's king,
A score such in his service.'
                              ' Go you, then,'
The knight rejoined, unmoved, 'and do your best
For England.   But, be sure, whate'er you do,
The king will aye undo it.   Monk will find
Himself of little worth whene'er the king
Shall seat him firmly.   I do truly think
His reign will be but evil.   We do know
Him better far than London's fickle crowd,
Or England love-sick of her late spurned rule.
Nay, prove me nevermore !   I am resolved !
I had to Breda, like to you, when first

Monk broached his project, had I purposed aught ;)
But you—well, here's my purse at comrade's need ?'

Thereafter stayed he little while.   But oft
His thoughts would homeward turn, his comrades gone ;
And that the more, some, mindful of him still,
Would send him greeting with well-meant reproof.

      *   *   *   *   *

One day a storm swept furious o'er the town,
And all the streets ran torrent-like with rain ;
Loud spake the thunder, while the lightning clave
The vault of heav'n to scorch the face of earth.
An ancient church stood ope, and shelter there
Sir Edward took, and, standing thoughtful, came
Upon him vision of Saint Bartlemy :
Rahere before the altar, kneeling low,
As last he saw her ere the angel flame
Touched her, and, touching, painless bare her home.

A thousand times remembrance had portrayed
The scene with grief-dipped pencil—ne'er as now.
All overcome, he reeled as one in wine,
And, clutching pillar, flung him down, and laid
His aching head against the pavement stone ;
While woke within him longing passionate,
Once more to gaze upon her tomb and die.

Not long thereafter, where the simple slab
Within the crumbling priory at home
Told of the guileless maid asleep beneath,
Long time a tall and stalwart soldier knelt

With lips compressed and down-bent head, and gaze
That worshipped ever the one word ' Rahere.'
Now plashed upon the slab a burning tear,
And now the lips unlocking, heart-breathed sigh,
' Rahere, Rahere !' swept sadly o'er the dead.
Then rose he and departed, yet as one
That must be gone unwilling, looking back
Continual, till arch and column hid
The founder's tomb, and where the maiden lay,
Rich gem in humble casket.
      Now without
The broken porch he crossed the dreary field,
And took him to the gate, her once abode.
Here passing under, turned he, as of old
Upgazing at the casement, where her face
Had smiled upon him, and her lustrous eyes—
Love's tell-tale orators—had fired his soul
Like coal from angel altar.
      ' I have done,
Dear love,' he sighed, ' such penance as before
None did nor can hereafter. Since I held
Thy little hand, no hand of womankind
Has lain in mine ; since last my greedy arms
Held thee, complacent prisoner of love,
Contemptuous all of lover use, they spurn
To fetter other, having fettered thee.
Mine eyes are blinded but to one sweet face,
Fairest of all the sinless sisterhood
That share thy bliss and bask amid thy smiles.
No voice may move me, save thine own whene'er
In dream I hear again thy sad farewell

And craving pity and forgiveness wake,
The music of thine accents agony
To sleep-deceived ears !   Where'er thou art,
Soul of my soul, so truly loved, behold
Thy grief-worn penitent, of very pain
Returned to worship at thy tomb, and speak
The peace all vainly sought in stranger lands.'
So murmured he, and out a dullard cloud
The westering sun shone forth, its slanting beam
Full on the blazoned casement that again
Cast down its burnished splendours and on him.
And with the gleam, as angel wing it were,
Love-charged for him with message from the dead,
Came blessed peace within his breast, as when
Some mother famished of her fear receives
News of her sailor darling 'scaped the storm.

And turning thence, mind-eased in wondrous wise,
His heart aglow with comfort long unknown
And sense of full forgiveness, from his lips
Brake, grateful, trembling : ' Am I then forgiv'n,
Sweet love, sweet love ?   Thy spirit, sure, did haunt
These rugged walls, and patient wait the day
Thy lover, passion-purged, should come again,
To speak him soul to soul, his penance done,
And breathe forgiveness ere ecstatic flight
Thou took'st to realms celestial, infinite.'

Now fell a shadow on him—rang the air
With cheery greeting, hearty welcoming :
' Sir Edward ! and Sir Edward home again !

Now God be praised ! But, lad, how broad and brown !
And, marry ! but Goliah's grip is thine !
Yet grip again and yet again.   I heard
Thou wouldst not back, and swore to seek thee out
Did but another laggard se'nnight pass,
And no word from thee.'
                   Thus the farrier Gould,
His honest face enkindling, and the more
He saw responsive light within the eyes
Of him he greeted.   ' Come, lad, in !   The gate
Is as thou left'st it.   First but look within
The stable.   See, Delight is—— Arrant fool
Am I to stir up trenchant memories !
Yet, see, the mare doth know thee.   Well done, lass !
Ay, ay ! thou hast thy master back again ;
Wilt bear him bravely yet, for all thy years.'

That night Sir Edward lay within the gate,
Guest to his humbler friend.   O'er foaming stoup,
Full oft replenished, sat they, till the dawn,
Graying the casement, chid loquacity.
Then rose the knight: ' To-morrow will I go
To Beech Hill, and the rather you affirm
Sir Giles tyrannic master.   Would, indeed,
Old Gilbert Hales did live !   Let them that will
Decry the dead !   To me was Cromwell friend,
And eke to him thereafter.   Like himself
It was to rate the rogues that sought to void
My deed of gift, well knowing it was made
Before malignancy,—convenient phrase,
Coined of the snatch-purse knaves to cover hate,

Revenge, and theft, and robbery of babes—
War-beggared of their sires—or hapless maids
And widows, weak and friendless, easy spoil.
But now good-night.   Yet supererogate
The wish in me for thee, thy wholesome thoughts,
Like spirit-children of thy mind, a guard
Impregnable about thee night and day !'

II.

Pale sentinel of thought, sleep negligent,
The knight withdrew, and, as his often wont,
Slow pacing watched the pearly face of Dawn
Flush roseate at the kissing of Dan Day,
Like lovely maid arrayed for holy rite,
That, innocent and pale with unknown fear,
Beholds her groom impatient at the gate
With priest and quire and merry minstrel train;
And, seeing, heeds no more till husband kiss,
Love's master-key, unlocks the realm of joy.

Soon shone the sun resplendent.   Through the pane
The bright beam leaped, like living spirit waked
Anew to bliss and blessing.   Chanticleer
From coop and cratch his shrilly challenge lift,
While out the dovecot poured melodious moan.
Beneath the eaves the sparrows, stirring, preened,
Then twittering forth bade God's new day good-day !
Fresh was the breeze that out the shadowy west
Came hastily at glimpsing of the Dawn,
To purge ere moil of day the turgid town

With wholesome odours out th' unsullied fields,
Benignant sucked from sleeping bud and bloom.

Erelong arose the carter's cheery song,
His fodder-wain, high piled from steamy stack,
Loud creaking through the gate, while all abroad
The long-pent fragrance fed the nearer gale.
Then rang the stithy anvil; first the vast
And wheezy bellows fanning languid flame
To fulgent fury, rageful spark, and roar.
So woke the town anew to healthy toil—
Mad mirth or dirge, dull base to bridal bells—
To cank'rous grief, that chid the smile of day
Or joy expectant, counting haste delay—
To all the tangling accidents of life,
Accursed of Fate or cheered by Fortune's smile.

Fair are thy fields, O England ! fair thy woods
That birth the breeze and draw the welcome shower,
Life-giving, out the fertile-bosomed cloud,
Down to the bright-hued children of their shade.
Fair are thy lanes, hedge-bordered, whether Spring,
Bemocking Winter's penance-sheet of snow,
Burgeons the fresh-leaved thorn, and all the way
O'erhangs with fragrant robe of creamy white ;
Or whether Summer bids the trailing bine
Its trumpet blossoms proffer, scattering blast
Sweet as Colombian gale that, o'er the main
Far-breathing, still the hidden isle betrays
Although the sailor vainly scan the sea ;
Or Autumn pranking out the sturdy briar

In livery of scarlet—wayfare tree
For comrade servitor, with trav'ler's joy
For plume amid their bonnets.   Fairer none
World over—nay, nor any half so fair !

So thought Sir Edward Hewett as he rode
Once more along the pleasant summer lanes,
Oft resting as some once familiar scene
Rose on his gaze delighted, either hand,
As wind of lane revealed, or crest of hill ;
Or, all unlooked-for opening 'mid the trees
Enticed the eye to where, reposeful, stood
Gray homestead, cot, or time-old sylvan hall.

' And I am home again, dear land !' he sighed,
' Who thought to come no more ; and every hour
I linger makes me half-heart denizen—
My every step but added link to chain
Of voluntary bondage.'   Thus the knight.
Nor long thereafter, when the mullioned hall,
His father's and his own, brake into view,
His heart sprang up, and all a-sudden stood
Hill, park, and hall obscured by misty veil.
The weakness past, he thoughtful rode until,
The road disparting—this toward the hall,
And this to Beechen Hadley and the green—
Delight unchidden of her rider took
The lodge-way track with ever-quick'ning stride,
As who would say, ' This way must be ; 'tis home !'
He gave her rein, sad smiling, nothing loath
Himself to view his boyhood home anear.
The gates were shut.   Delight, impatient, neighed,

And at the sound came forth a stranger dame,
Who, curtseying, stood uncertain.
                                    ' Who is now
The master at the Hall ?' Sir Edward asked,
By way of pretext for intrusiveness.
'Sir Giles Fitzwarren, please your honour.   But
There is himself a-coming.'
            .   O'er the space,
Betwixt the gate and beechen avenue,
There came a man age-bent, on potence staff,
Who, formal courtesy past, his pleasure bade.
Then said the knight : ' I am but lately come
From France—all loyal Englishmen to home—
Had there Sir Edward Hewett's only son
For comrade—him that should be master here.
Nay, frown not at the name, Sir Giles.   Himself
Reluctant to return, nor half resolved,
Did bid me come of friendship, proffer terms
Full honourable to both, but most to you.
An he should come, what say you? Will you yield
Possession on fair purchase ?'
                                    Thus the knight
To adversary, generous.   Churlish he
Made answer hasty : ' Time enough for terms
Sir Edward home.   No busy go-between
I suffer ! 'Tis my answer ! Sir, good-day !'
So snarled he through the bars.   Sir Edward smiled,
Then, careless, bowed and turned Delight away.

'So had I said, Sir Giles Fitzwarren, I !
Well, well, 'twould seem a spell is on the place.

Niggard succeeding niggard ! There's the lake !
And there the willow dangling as of yore,
Its withy screen before the traitor's hole,
And rustling ghostly as the pallid shade
Of him that hideous, struggling, shook the tree
In death-throe penalty for treachery,
Did haunt for evermore his place of doom !'
Thus he, recalling tale of Barons' war.
And after : ' Ay, there's gold enough to buy
The place thrice over, should it yet be hid.'
A grassy way, with vault of pendent ash,
And panelling of maple broader grown
To bosquet hedge, led up to comely farm.
The gate wide ope, he rode within the yard,
And, halting, called a name in stentor tone.
A hale old man came forward.   First the knight
He eyed full sharply, then Delight, and then
Gave forth a shout : ' Sir Edward !   Boys, the squire !
The squire—God bless him !—home to cheer us all !'
Then brake his voice, nor more could say, but wept.

Soon seated 'twixt the farmer and his dame,
Whose sturdy sons stood bashful nigh, while oft
A shout went up without, and eager eyes
Gleamed at the casement or the part-closed door,
Sir Edward felt a novel pleasure wake
Within his breast, and chide what lingered yet
Of morbid self-excision.   Soon he spake :
' I did not think to have such welcoming,
Old friend and friends ; I left you when a boy,
Despairing, reckless, mindful but of self.'

' Nay, nay, Sir Edward ! Nay, we heard the tale,'
The farmer brake in quickly ; ' not a heart
But bled to hear it. Yet 'twas foreordained,
And long ago. God rest the maiden's soul !
You must aback and wed a proper mate.
My dame doth bless you night and day for thought,
In all the harass of your own distress,
Of us, and what might follow Worcester fight.
We had the gold of Hales, and but for that,
With murrain, blight, and double rent, had lost
The homestead, been adrift to starve or steal.'

Surprised Sir Edward heard. Then came to mind
His charge to Gilbert not to spare the store,
Occasion needing. This recalled, he smiled,
And answered with intention : ' Friend, of that
We'll more anon, what time, restored, I ask
Accompt of Gilbert.'
                             ' Nay, the steward's dead,'
The old man answered gravely.
                                   ' So I heard
Last night from Gould the farrier. Also this :
Young Hales doth hold a stead at Totteridge,
Cock Fosters sold a year or so agone.
Some message he for me will surely hold,
Perchance some papers.'
                             ' Ay, the steward left
Three such, for fear they should mischance. Here's one !
Ha, ha ! the old man knew his men ! For all
My debt he came, and harboured one with me.
Right glad am I the first to give accompt.'

So chuckling, rose the farmer from his seat,
And now, unlocking banded chest of oak,
With ponderous key that slid an inner bolt
Back from its hasp with shock that shook the chest,
Took out a broadsheet letter.   This the knight,
Perusing slowly, read of steadfast worth
And true devotion.   How the gold was safe,
Its caverned hiding-place to none revealed ;
How yet from time to time, as need arose
Among the tenants, mostly from the greed
Of their new master, something from the store
He warily had taken, so the love
He bare his master they might doubly bear,
Whom yet he friended, absent !   Followed prayer
For quick return, before his aged eyes
Shut on the world without the solace balm
Of smile or tear from long-desirèd face.

A schedule of the sums so timely lent
Accompanied the letter.   This the knight
Put by unread.   ' Now, Gilbert, mayst thou rest
In peace for pattern of an honest man !'
He said, much moved, the while he put away
The papers in his doublet.   Yet an hour
He stayed ; Delight, a crowd about her stall,
Regaling of the best, then took the road,
Far followed by a shouting from the farm,
To Totteridge and the stead of younger Hales.

Of purpose riding slow along the green,
Each memorable feature either hand
Bidding delay, or courting second look,

A-sudden swept the music of the bells
The beacon belfry out, melodious roar
That filled the air and bade the swaying woods,
Blend all their myriad murmurings in the strain.
An urchin passing by : 'Why ring the bells?
Good lad, canst tell me?'
                        Quick the boy replied,
Touching his forelock : 'Sir, the squire is home,
Sir Edward Hewett, him that went away
To fight Old Noll at Worcester.   When 'tis night,
'Tis said they'll fire the beacon.'   Thus the lad,
And bounded off to tell the mighty news
To comrades seen against the hither wood.

And deep within the lonesome wanderer's breast
The music sinking thousand echoes woke
Responsive to its pleading.   'Here is home,'
Again and yet again each swirling bell
In clamorous persistence seemed to say,
'With honest hearts that love you.   Wand'rer, stay
Man's truest mate is duty.   Grief for loss
Too long indulged is triple loss, that doth
But wreck the present in the stormy past,
And cloud the future with respicient pain.'

*   *   *   *   *

His task benign to grateful Terra done,
The Sun his empire orb began to veil
In fleece of gold that, slow descending, sank
Ablaze with proud effulgence to the main.
And couched upon a bank within a wood—
A sunny bank where purpling tufts of thyme

Wedded the sward—Sir Edward thoughtful lay,
Escaped awhile from welcomings that grew
Almost to weariness.
                         A scroll lay near
In bed of alehoof, whose disparted whorls
Gave out reproachful fragrance for the rude
And unredressed intrusion.   At his feet—
Of instinct made a friend within an hour—
A hound stretched out his nozzle o'er his paws,
And drowsy waited.   Through the quivering leaves
The red light danced, to gild the restless boughs
That waved loquacious in the wakening breeze,
Or flush the bole of some mound monarch tree
With lingering kiss at parting.
                                    Overhead
The rooks sailed, weary, homeward, often caw
Encheering stragglers onward.   Not enough
Of his sweet freight encargasoned, the bee
Hummed loud, one last load seeking ere his home
He sought complacent.   Evensong the birds
In chorus lifted, till some nearer mate,
Song-frenzied and to passion-rapture fired,
Shook all the wood, and, thrilling heart and ear,
Attuned the list'ner's soul to sympathy.

' Ah, God, how happy all Thy world but man !
And he Thine image !   Is it, Lord, that we
Do err in seeking happiness on earth ?
Our other, larger home—Thy home—the goal
Of all our aims, our only blessedness.'
So murmured he, what time the woodland lay,

A moment stilled, brake forth again more near.
'Though sorrow make us wise, and stripes do bring
The errant soul again to wisdom's way,
What need of stripe or sorrow?   All men 'Thine,
To do with as Thou wilt from crib to grave.'
So he, again pursuing danger thought,
The while the bird melodious jubilance
Lift up to heaven.   Now strangely, deeply moved,
All of a moment through his earnest soul
The thought flashed, 'I will trust Him though He slay.'
Almost beyond his purpose or his will
The thought had birth ; but birthed, it thrilled him
     through
And through beyond all telling.
                              To his lips
The words welled up, then faltering died, as died
The feathered song, a footstep falling nigh.
Now rose the shaggy hound, and lazy shook
His tawny hide, but not as waked to wrath,
For, whining low, he left the soldier's side
To greet more proved acquaintance.   Down the knoll,
The devious path forsaken, came a maid
Faultlessly fair, as fabled she that won
The slighted Goddess' discord gift.   Adown
Her snow-white bodice fell her raven hair,
Glossy as jet.   Her rounded cheek the sun
Had kissed to summer ripeness, while her lips
Aparted, as with eager upturned gaze
She list the linnet's song, were red as hip
That, touched of Autumn's vermeil fingers, fires
The hedgerow.   Parted thus, their ivory store

Were plain to view, contented prisoners
To such rare gaoler mistress. Lithe her form,
And supple as the willow herb in wind,
With dainty feet that out her woodland dress
Stood fearless on the sward. As brought again
To earth from music's nearer heav'n at whine
Of welcoming hound, she stayed her in surprise.

Sir Edward hasty rose. She showed no fear,
But queenly stood; but he, he trembling gazed
Wide-eyed, and all his oft-proved bravery gone.
' Rahere !' he faltered, then again, ' Rahere !'
While in his look dread strove with love, and all
The fibres of his manhood were unstrung.

But at the name the maiden's face grew sad ;
Her eyes, like crystal founts, welled o'er with tears,
While tremor after tremor shook her form.
' Rahere !' she softly murmured, then more loud,
But still with trembling accent : ' Sir, you name
One long since dead—my sister !' Here distress
Sometime imprisoned speech.
                              He now, assured
To find the maid no spirit as at first
He deemed, came forward : ' Lady, ot a truth,
I took you for unearthly visitant,
Yet not unwelcome—shade of noble maid,
Short known, quick lost, but loved with loyal love
Through years of exile, danger, and distress !
She had a sister, fondly loved, of whom

She spake me often.   You are surely she—
So like herself, my heart 'twixt fear and love
Leapt up tumultuous, greeting, fearing still.'

Now smiled the maiden through her tears, her hand
Stretched forth in fearless innocence, and locked
Fast in his swarthier palm.   ' I am Cecile,'
She answered ; then more hastily, ' and you
Sir Edward Hewett !   All the tale is writ
For ever in my heart.   You loved Rahere—
Forgive me, I do never speak the name
But needs must weep—you loved her, and for love
Of her, so cruel snatched away of Death,
Did guardian me, her sister, sisterless—
A child you ne'er had known !   'Twas but of late
I knew my benefactor !   This mid-day
I heard the bells at Hadleigh, and was told
Sir Edward had returned.   Ah me ! how oft
At night your name has mingled with the names
I lay before the orphans' God and Friend,
With prayer for safe return and happiness !
Will you not take again the gold you left
In trust for me ?   I would have sent it o'er
The seas, but could not, being child.   But now
Take back your gift.   My uncle yester-eve
Said you were poor, Sir Giles unlike to yield
Your heritage save only at the cost
Of weary suit.   'Twill help you to your own,
Be sure, as giv'n of Godlike charity
To helpless child, more surely than the wealth
Of Crœsus were it ready laid to hand.'

Surprised he heard, then gravely spake her back :
' 'Tis writ that "they that sow in tears shall reap
In joy," and so I prove it.   Yet, sweet child,
Believe me, I have never need of gold.
I am not poor ; have wealth enough to buy
Twice over and to spare mine own again.
Yet o'er and o'er I thank you.   You do show
In truth your sister's sister.   So am I
A thousandfold repaid for deed forgot !'

The farms adjoined.   Without the wood a path
O'er meadow-croft and cornland took Cecile,
He by her side to eager questioning
As eagerly replying, stile and gap
Made easy by sustent of manly hand.
She home, he made to turn him back again,
But stayed, her hand laid quick upon his arm.
' Nay, be our guest a little while,' she said,
With sweet entreaty.   ' Uncle is within.
I have so much to say of gratitude,
That he will better say ; but could you read
My heart, no tongue were half so eloquent !'

She, reading in his eyes ungrudged assent,
Went joyous, hasty in, with sparkling eyes,
To bear the news.   Soon came the farmer out
With dame and maids obsequious.   Honoured guest
That night he lay beneath the homestead eaves,
A message sent in haste across the fields.
But first, Othello-like, of war and 'scape
Spell-bound his hearers.   She, Cecile, on whom

His eye delighted dwelled continual, sat
A little way removed, her royal head
Laid close against the good-wife's matron breast.
But oft her eyes would seek the soldier's face,
And aye encountering smiling gaze, revealed,
Sweet innocent, in answering smile, the love
Waking within her.
                        He the ache of years
Felt lessen every instant. She so like
The cherished image of his thought, the Past
In presence of her beauty grew to dream ;
While in her smile the sorrow-cloud, so long
Enshrouding in its fold his nobler self,
Melted apace, as melts the ghostly mist
That haunts the chalkland after summer rain,
In fire of living sunbeam chasing storm.

III.

The hidden gold regained, Sir Edward soon,
On miser terms, his own acquired again.
Came Yuletide round, and all the countryside
Flocked to the wide-thrown hall, while loud the bells
Gave forth their brazen melody, nor knew
Repose till night forbade their noisy joy.

Fair was the tide, the red sun's level beams
Soothing the rigorous air, whose fang of late
Had prisoned brook and lake. The hedgedrift snow
Shone in the radiance, while each frosted bough

And branch gleamed faery white, or, breeze-touched,
    shook
From time to time their glistering burthen down.

Loud rang the bells, but ne'er for lovelier maid
Than she who plighted bridal troth to-day!
Bright shone the sun, but ne'er on sweeter face
Than hers who, now led blushing to her place
Beside her morn-made groom, ordained the feast
Begin with all its merriment and cheer.
True dame henceforth of loyal lord—whose heart,
Of suffering tuned to sympathy with pain,
Knew never joy like that which, Godlike, brings
Relief to him that needs—sat now Cecile,
Sweet cynosure of all.
              A little while,
And one uprose. 'Twas Gould, most honoured guest,
And, cup in hand, bade silence while he gave
A toast all hearts repeated. ' Drink we now
His honour and his lady !'
              Rang the hall
With tenant tumult, while the worthier came
To kiss the little hand that, trembling, first
Was lifted up to lips of smiling spouse.
Then spake she softly : ' You that know my heart
As I, or better, Edward, husband, speak
These, and for me, as I would speak them could
But simple tongue reveal o'erchargèd heart.'

This did he, facund made of gratitude
For evil haply past, and love of her
That breathless hung entranced upon his lips.

'Yet one thing more,' he said, his speech to end,
And out his bridal vest drew slowly forth
The schedule of his people's debtedness
As writ by Gilbert.   This in sight of all
He cast upon the flames that lapped the log—
The jolly Yule-log bickering on the hearth—
And calmly watched it burn itself away.
'Though done with mine, the deed was his the more
Who, faithful ever, stood for me, although
The sea between us rolled, and love alone
O'er-bridged the gulf with plank of tender hope—
Denied, alas !—that day as this might glad
His aged eyes before he sank to sleep !
Repay him, then, as he would be repaid,
Did he but live to speak it, friends, by love
Of her this day, bride blushing in your midst,
Your lady and mine own, Cecile, my wife !'

Then shouted they again, till all the hall
Shook with their shouting, roof and corridor
Reverberant with honest English cheer.
She meanwhile, happy maid, her lovelit eyes
Lift lustrous to her lord's, whose ardent gaze
Scarce dared she to sustain, yet, brave of love,
Met and returned, while into his her hand
Slid trustful.   Thus she stood before her folk
The noblest, fairest, dearest, in the land.

THE END.

Elliot Stock, Paternoster Row, London.

www.ingramcontent.com/pod-product-compliance
Lightning Source LLC
Chambersburg PA
CBHW030353270326
41926CB00009B/1083